"Finally! A comprehensible, easy to follow, succinct and knowledgeable book on the casting process. This is a 'must read' for anyone in the industry, whether they are involved in the casting process or not."
— Kari Wishingrad, producer and actress: *Just Under A Million, The Perfect Kiss Goodnight, Twine*

"There can *never* be too much good information about the casting process! Read and learn!"
— Sarah Kliban, casting director, San Francisco – International Talent Casting: *Milk, All About Evil*, NBC's *Trauma*

"Buy this book! Your meticulously interwoven match-ups, brilliant roller-coaster dolly shots and pricey aerial long shots will not save your poorly cast film. For years filmmaker, director, producer and casting director Hester Schell has shared her knowledge and expertise with clients, directors, friends, students and colleagues. At long last she has put her words on paper. I am so pleased to hold this book."
— Candy Campbell, author and filmmaker: *How Low Can You Go?*

"I wish there had been a book like this out there when I directed my first feature. Of course I had the next best thing. I had Hester. My advice to directors is this: When you cast your film, think in terms of a camping trip. Would you want to go camping for an extended amount of time with this person? Attitude and personality will always win out over talent and looks."
— Robert Pickett, writer and director: *Sydney Town The Musical, The Divine Madness, The Deli.*

"This book is a master class for actors and filmmakers. This will be required reading for all of my students, and if you are thinking about making a film or acting in a film, I recommend that you read *Casting Revealed* first. The entire process of filmmaking has so many layers and subtleties, any one of which can create incredible headaches and heartaches if the process is not followed with precision. The entire production is executed like a ballet, and without a clear understanding of the dance you are facing artistic and financial disaster."
— Stephen Kopels, director, PBS producer, founder – San Francisco School of Digital Filmmaking

"Hester Schell has put together an excellent resource for directors, producers and new actors. The information contained in this book is smart, clear and concise; it steers the reader from some common pitfalls one might encounter when choosing and working with actors — be it union or non-union. Everything is well covered here, from casting breakdowns and 'attracting the talent' to the audition process and dealing with unions and contracts. It's a must-have for anyone embarking on a new film or video. Bravo!"
— Nanci Gaglio, award-winning writer and director, co-creator/executive producer: *Venus Rising*, BBC

"When constructing a project as huge and difficult as a feature film, you need to have your tool belt filled with the equipment that will ensure that your project has the greatest chance of success, and the knowledge of the casting process is a tool no director can live without. Hester Schell's book will help you turn your gibberish into positive and confident communication, and get you started on the right path to a successful and enjoyable casting experience. Don't make a movie without reading this book. You'll be happy you did, and so will your actors."
— Paul Martin, DGA director

"This tool for our industry is a gift to anyone who spends Penny One on a production. We all benefit from Hester's knowledge and candor, which emanates from the vast first-hand experience of a well-educated professional."
— Kari Nevil, CEO – June Bug Films, director: *Planting Melvin, Your Guardian*

"Hester Schell knows the film production process inside and out, in front of and behind the camera. And she's an accomplished acting teacher. Whether you're a neophyte performer or have a mile-long resume, you will improve your auditions using her vital information."
— Don Schwartz, actor, contributing writer – *CineSource* magazine

"For many filmmakers, casting is a nebulous, confusing process... yet thanks to Hester Schell, writers and directors now have an arsenal of easy-to-use tools with which to plan their casting sessions and to communicate to actors exactly what they're looking for. Finding the right performers to bring your characters to life is no easy task. Thanks to *Casting Revealed*, it just got a bit easier."
— Chad Gervich, writer/producer: *Wipeout, Speeders, Foody Call, Reality Binge*; author: *Small Screen, Big Picture: A Writer's Guide to the TV Business*

"A much-needed book for independent filmmakers. There are so many books out there about directing and writing, etc., that it's great to see a book cover this other crucial aspect of getting a film made — how to go about casting the right people. By giving both an overview of the casting process for those new to it, as well as information for those already involved, this will help you to avoid making mistakes and casting the wrong people."
— Erin Corrado, *onemoviefiveviews.com*

"For independent directors looking for a guide to help in the casting process, Hester Schell provides one hell of an interesting little book that lays out all of the steps in bringing aboard the right actors for your project... allow[ing] the reader to cut through the crap and get down to the nitty gritty of the entire process. For anyone interested in a serious look into casting, check out this book."
— Felix Vasquez Jr., *Cinema Crazed*

"When an actor walks into your audition, a director needs to find out three things immediately: Do they look the part? Do they have range? Can they take direction? Hester Schell has written an invaluable book on the casting process that answers those questions, plus she gives you the tools you need to run a proper casting session and tips on how to make the actors feel safe."
— Peter D. Marshall, director, instructor – Vancouver Film School

"A gem of a book... please read it before you launch your next film project and enjoy the success it surely will bring."
— Celik Kayalar, founder and program director – Film Acting Bay Area

"This new, direct, and friendly volume will demystify the casting process. Hester talks the talk because she has walked the walk. Casting is a mystery no more."
— Michael Helmy, producer

"Selecting the right actors for a film is probably among the most critical things a filmmaker can do. Hester Schell puts the art and process of casting into a clear perspective. It's a very useful guide for any producer or director and will help set a film in the right direction from the very start. This should be required reading for any first-time filmmaker, and even old pros will find this valuable."
— Steve Michelson, Executive Producer – Lobitos Creek Ranch Productions

CASTING REVEALED

HESTER SCHELL

a guide for film directors

MICHAEL WIESE PRODUCTIONS

Published by Michael Wiese Productions
12400 Ventura Blvd. #1111
Studio City, CA 91604
(818) 379-8799, (818) 986-3408 (FAX)
mw@mwp.com
www.mwp.com

Actress on cover: Rebecca Grant
Cover photograph: Brigitte Jouxtel
Cover design by Johnny Ink. www.johnnyink.com
Interior design by William Morosi
Printed by McNaughton & Gunn

Manufactured in the United States of America
Copyright 2010 by Hester Schell

Library of Congress Cataloging-in-Publication Data

Schell, Hester D.
 Casting revealed : a guide for film directors / by Hester Schell.
    p. cm.
 Includes bibliographical references and index.
 ISBN 978-1-932907-87-2
 1. Motion pictures--Casting. I. Title.
 PN1995.9.C34S34 2011
 791.43'0233--dc22
                                          2010030971

Mixed Sources
Product group from well-managed
forests and other controlled sources
www.fsc.org Cert no. SW-COC-002283
© 1996 Forest Stewardship Council

This book is dedicated to anyone who has ever made a good movie and wants to make a great movie, for you already know it is essential to hire great actors.

CONTENTS

CHAPTER THREE:
AN OVERVIEW OF THE CASTING PROCESS...14

CHAPTER SEVEN:
THE CASTING BREAKDOWN — SPREADING THE WORD

CHAPTER EIGHT:
STAYING ORGANIZED

CHAPTER NINE:
THE FIRST ROUND — WHAT YOU NEED AND WHERE YOU NEED IT

ACKNOWLEDGEMENTS

My experiences in acting, directing, teaching and casting have all contributed to the processes and procedures shared in this book.

I wish to extend very special thanks to these friends and artists who have helped with various particulars during the process: Polly Bray, Erika and Sebastian Degens, Karen Shepard, Phil Gorn, Robert Pickett, Jan Powell, Mary Trainor-Brigham, Stephanie Carwin, Maxine Greco, Mary Garcia, Shawn-Caulin Young, Fred Pitts, André Mathieu, Kari Nevil, Stephen Kopels, Paul Martin, Scott Anderson and the Harvard Square Screen Writers group, and casting directors Tamara McDaniel, CSA, Ken Lazer in New York City, and Sarah Kliban in San Francisco. Thank you, Candy Campbell and Annie-Scott Rogers for insisting I get busy and start writing. You are truly great friends. To Kari Wishingrad, who was there with coaching when I needed it. To my mother, who knew I was a writer before I did. Very special thanks and appreciation to my proofreader and first-draft editor, Kelly Thompson. My supreme thanks to the editorial staff at Michael Wiese Productions: Matt Barber and William Morosi, Ken Lee, and my publisher, Michael Wiese. It is truly an honor to be among the distinguished writers at Michael Wiese Books.

HESTER'S PERSPECTIVE

BY CANDY CAMPBELL

The casting process can be the belly of the beast... or the armor that protects it. The decisions you are about to make will decide the fate of your film and quite possibly your physical well-being for the next months and years. An insolent statement? Hear me out. Beware: if you think that filmmaking is more art than business, you're 50% wrong. The behemoth of filmmaking is simultaneously 100% art and 100% business.

Casting can be the causative agent for one of the longest-running migraines a filmmaker will ever endure. If you take the quick and easy way out, your migraine will surely become a constant affliction, and your film will suffer a paralyzing, convulsive, demise. Your meticulous interwoven match-ups, brilliant roller coaster dolly shots and pricey aerial long shots will not save your poorly cast film. Your film-child's remains will be flung on the dung heap of miserable, rotting plastic, with all the other miserable, rotting dreams of filmmaker-wannabes, littering the landfill. And you will be wishing the remains were more biodegradable.

"The Ghost Of Past Project Failed" will make you a pariah at producer networking and extended family events. How many years will it take until your one-time fans, who reached into their pockets to help you, can look you in the eye? You'll *wish* it were a dream, but it's more like the nightmare-leaking faucet that eventually causes the flood. But wait! There, at the end of the tunnel, a dim flicker. Is it a train? No! It is your way out of this hole. It is... this book! For years, my friend, filmmaker, director, producer and casting director, Hester Schell, has shared her knowledge and expertise with clients, director friends, students and colleagues. She has, at long last, put her words on paper. I am so pleased, at long last, to hold this book. Now, go forth. Create. And do the earth a favor. Lighten the landfills. Read and absorb the contents of this book. Did I forget something? Oh, yes. Buy this book!

Candy Campbell

Candy Campbell is an actress, comedienne, author, filmmaker and registered nurse who made her television debut on NBC's *Trauma*. Ms. Campbell produced and directed the award-winning documentary film, *Micropremature Babies: How Low Can You Go?* (*candycampbell.com*). Her book, *My Mom Is A Nurse*, is available at Amazon.

SOMETHING ABOUT HER

BY ROBERT PICKETT

I first met Hester Schell working on *Entertaining Mr. Sloan*, by Joe Orton. Hester brilliantly played my sister, and we had a blast. She came to the University of Utah for the graduate directing program in the theatre department in the late 1980s. We would embark on a lifelong friendship that would find us supporting, encouraging, auditioning, acting, directing, producing, teaching, touring, and, for a short time, living together, over the next 20 years.

We have worked together on many productions and have taught classes in the San Francisco Bay Area for film directors and actors. We have sorted headshots and resumes, sat through auditions and interviews, hired crews and scouted locations. Through it all, I have come to realize that Hester knows what she's talking about. She's been there through every phase of the creative process and has a keen understanding of what makes a film idea turn into a film.

My advice to directors is this: When you cast your film or a play, think in terms of a camping trip. Would you want to go camping for an extended amount of time with this person? Because you need to be sure it's a "Yes." You will be spending a lot of time with this person and you want to know: would they help fetch water, clean the campsite, help start a fire, cook a meal, carry wood or sing as we sat around a campfire roasting marshmallows? Attitude and personality will always win out over talent and looks. Some of the greatest actors are the greatest people and no amount of talent can replace a great attitude or helpful disposition on a set. Trust your instincts. I can usually tell within the first thirty seconds of an audition, and sometimes even before an audition starts, if an actor is right for the role or the production. Always think in terms of the big picture and not what may seem at the time as an attractive quality or charming smile.

This book can help both the person new to filmmaking and the person who has had a difficult time with past productions to avoid the pitfalls along the journey.

The only other advice I would give you is to find a "Hester" and keep them close in your life. Someone who will always tell you the truth, share your agonies and your ecstasies; someone who knows more than you do about the business.

Break a leg!

Robert Pickett, MFA
Fair Oaks, California

Robert Pickett is a native Californian, teacher, director, performer, screenwriter and playwright. He is the author of numerous screenplays and is currently working on *Sydney Town*, a musical in development about San Francisco at the height of the gold rush, based on characters and stories from the book *The Barbary Coast* by Herbert Asbury, author of *The Gangs of New York*. His most recent project is the play *Deli,* a modern retelling of *King Lear* that takes place in an Italian-American delicatessen in San Francisco's North Beach neighborhood. He is the founder of Napa Valley Shakespeare Festival.

INTRODUCTION

You've heard it all your life: There is no trying, only doing. It's true. The world is full of folks who only try, folks who get it wrong every step of the way. You probably have worked for some of them. Maybe at one time you were one of those people. But you're smarter now. You picked up this book. So, let's get started.

This book is about the casting process, actors and acting. This book will help you to spot new talent, weed out the "wannabes" and run professional casting sessions. This book will inform and guide you through the preproduction specifics necessary for finding the best actors for the characters in your movie. It will help you become better at running professional auditions and to navigate through such things as agents, contracts and the performers' unions.

This is not a book about how to finalize your script, although I suggest you get a few second and third opinions from people who know story structure and character. This is not a book about film production, although many aspects of the production process will be discussed. This is not a book about great lighting, although I recommend that you know enough about what a gaffer does to know you need a really good one. This is not a book about makeup and wardrobe or art direction or production design. Although, you guessed it: I recommend that you know enough to hire artists who can help you make the best movie you can make, regardless of your budget. In a world where anyone thinks they can make a movie, this book has finally found its time.

To get the most out of this book, I will make a few assumptions:

- You know something about filmmaking's five stages:
  Development (script)
  Preproduction (casting and planning the shoot)
  Production (on-set shooting)
  Postproduction (editing)
  Distribution (sales, marketing and film festivals)
- You know you are embarking on a long-term project with a few inherent certainties, the very least of which is basic organizational and computer skills, and impeccable communication skills. I've seen many a project get off on the wrong foothold for lack of good phone and email etiquette, being disrespectful of people's time, and not staying on top of procedures.

And finally...

- No more assumptions. Never assume anyone has any idea what you're talking about. Never assume your staff sees the same picture in their heads that you see in yours. So, go for the storyboards. Go for rehearsal. It's important to be ready to rock and... roll camera.

A director I've worked with who has made it to numerous festivals with her features wears a T-shirt on-set that says "Just Make The Movie." Another friend, a producer who has worn more hats than anyone I know says, "at the end of the day, or the end of your life, would you have rather made the movie or be sitting around wishing you'd made the movie?"

So here you are. With a script you like. Perhaps one you wrote. Or maybe a friend wrote it, and she's got a decent camera and you've agreed that you are going to make the movie. Another friend says he can do the lighting, and someone else shows up on sound. You have a skeleton crew, some resources, and someone took a film production class. Add it all up, and the universe is screaming at you: "Make The Movie!" I'm telling you too: "Make The Movie!" — and make it great! At the end of the day, you'll be glad to sit in a darkened theatre at a film festival, watching your story up there on the screen, taking the audience on your adventure. Give it all you've got. Do your very best to finish it. Do your very best to get it into the film festivals that count. Always, in everything you do, do your best to get it right.

Good luck on your project.

See you on-set!

Hester Schell
Half Moon Bay, California

CHAPTER 1

SAVE MONEY – DO IT YOURSELF

"It's an entirely new paradigm where a film made for $15,000 can co-exist as a theatrical feature alongside one made for over $300 million." — DAVID WORTH on *Paranormal Activity* and *Avatar*

"I let the actors work out their ideas before shooting, then tell them what attitudes I want. If a scene isn't honest, it stands out like a sore thumb."
— DAVID LYNCH

Directors Speak: In Session

❝ Casting often comes down to the most minute of details. If the leading woman I want most needs to be X inches shorter than our leading man, my decision is almost made for me. Does one actor seem easier to work with? Does one actor have more experience? How much will I have to direct this person? Does this person take direction? ❞

■ ■ ■ ■ ■

❝ Being 'right for the role' is how you get the part. Always. And that doesn't just mean looking and sounding like an archetype for the character you'd be playing. It means that all of the factors a director considers, even the superficial ones, work in your favor — in the subjective opinion of the director. That is what makes you 'right' for the role, and that is why you would land it. Casting is 90% of a director's work, and if you have the right cast, most of your job is done. If the director has cast people who are right for each role, the production will be successful, and the majority of people will agree with the casting. Casting your brother's nephew because he is your brother's nephew is obviously one of those factors a director should not be considering, for if your brother's nephew is right for the role because of his familial ties, most people will probably see that, and it will come back to haunt you. ❞

INDEPENDENT MARKET SHARE

Americans love movies. According to ShowBIZ Data, the United States box office share in 2009 was a whopping 40.4%. The rest of the world took the remaining 59.6%. While everyone debates changes to the delivery method, whether via theaters, computers, phones, or other yet-to-be-invented gadgets, Americans will continue to seek cinematic entertainment. What is really interesting is how much more market share the independent filmmakers are taking.

2009 U.S. MARKET SHARES (FROM SHOWBIZ DATA)

Distributor	Gross (in billions)	Share
WARNER BROS.	2,009	18%
20TH CENTURY FOX	1,480	13%
SONY	1,351	12%
BVI	1,268	11%
PARAMOUNT	1,050	9%
OTHERS	4,150	36%
TOTAL	11,398	

Paramount lost big in 2009. Notice the "Others" at the bottom of the list with a whopping 36% of the market. That is us: the other distributors and the independents making up 36% of the market, and rising.

Here's another interesting fact, from *The Economist*, March 13-19, 2010, page 33. According to Amy Lemisch, director of the California Film Commission: "California's world share of studio films (i.e., those made by the six biggest studios) dropped from 66% in 2003 to 35% in 2008."

Low-budget independent movies are becoming the bulk of the film industry. Looking at box office receipts, the studios and big distributors are top money dog. But looking at the total numbers of films made which were accepted into festivals, and you will find every festival jammed with low-budget independent films in a feeding frenzy to win anything, garner attention ("buzz") and move up the food chain toward distribution deals. Studio executives scour the festivals in search of the moneymaker. And they find them. The cream rises to the top with great writing, great casting, great direction and camerawork.

Movies are made on "speculation" nowadays. It is very similar to how a real estate broker, a builder and an architect build "spec" houses, recouping building costs at the time of sale for their return on investment (ROI).

Moviemaking is a lot of hard work and casting is just one more preproduction sequence to complete. So let's get started. You have a story to tell. You have a vision and you think it's original, and no one else has done it yet — Well, not exactly the way you see it. Always remember that: the way you see it. And you want to have a good time making it. And get to the festivals. And recoup your costs, and hopefully win some awards, so your next movie will be better funded. And so it goes.

Perhaps you've researched the demographics and know that the action-loving 18-to-24-year-old Asian male watches more movies than anyone else on the planet, and you want a piece of that pie. Or maybe you've noticed recently how well vampire movies are doing, and want to take a stab at a teen-slasher movie, or a romantic comedy, or a period drama. Maybe your uncle left you 50 acres in Montana with some horses, which is a great location for a western. You did your homework and discovered that one of the last great westerns was *Brokeback Mountain*, and you figure, "Why not me? I can make a movie about the American West." Ang Lee thought so too, and he's from Taiwan.

HOW THIS BOOK WILL SAVE YOU MONEY

Do it yourself.

The most important part about making a great movie is starting with a great script. This book is about the second most important part: actors. Too often we simply forget to allow enough time to find the perfect actors for the movie. Since there are plenty of actors to choose from, and often casting is done at the last minute, sometimes plenty of great people do show up. However, if you plan to cast in the spring for a summer shoot, and you want really good up-and-coming actors with "buzz," you will need to plan ahead. There are many things you can do yourself, and save on casting fees. There will come a time and place when you will certainly need to hire a casting professional. But for your small cast, simple location feature or short, you can learn how to do most of it yourself. And if you've already been doing most of it yourself, you will learn from your mistakes and get better at it. It's all about your communication skills as the director, the visionary of the project.

Because you will be able to do the headshot sorting, appointment arranging and screening out of the undesirable applicants yourself, you will save time and money on casting. You will also learn why, and under what circumstances, to hire a casting director.

Collaborate or die.

Moviemaking is truly a collaborative process. To save money, it is essential to get more done in less time and get it done right. You will spend much more time in preproduction, yet only weeks in production shooting. Avoiding reshoots requires professionals to be onboard in every aspect of the collaboration. Directors spend a lot of time pondering shot lists and filters and forget to spend sufficient time looking for qualified, eager, talented, capable, enthusiastic and trained actors. They are out there. You just have to know where to look and what to do when you find them.

Anyone can make a movie.

Better cameras are available with technology that didn't exist even two years ago. Because the financial barriers to making a good movie are breaking down, low-budget movies are becoming the industry standard. As we watch the studios lose more market share, and innovative, independent producers reinvent the funding process, good films are getting made in extraordinarily creative ways. Unknown actors are thrust into the spotlight and new careers are launched. For example, look at what happened in 2009 with Gabourey Sidibe in *Precious: Based on the Novel 'Push' by Sapphire* — instant stardom, plucked from obscurity by one life-changing audition.

When you have motivated and inspiring actors in a role, enthused about where they are and what they are doing, most of your shoot days will be easy and fun and your decisions will be about where to put the lens to capture these wonderful performances and whether to go for another take that's even better than the safety shot you just got! Wouldn't that be a dream?

Whether you are a new or seasoned director, assistant or executive producer learning as much as you can, organizing and running a better casting process will get you on your way toward making better movies. And who wouldn't want to make a better movie? We all want to get to the festival, get the distribution deal, and have our work seen in theaters nationally and internationally.

Yes, but is it worth watching?

Anyone can make a movie. Sure! But is it worth watching? There's a huge difference between a "vanity" project — a hobbyist who has money to burn, wants to star and has some friends he's convinced to fund this adventure — and a film that is well-crafted (as in good production values), captivates, resonates and thrills an audience.

Why so many films don't make the film festivals.

In general, low-budget films fail to get into festivals for three reasons: weak story, acting or production quality. Film festival juries are keen to high production value. When juries screen films for festivals they watch about the first 15 minutes. If anything appears off about production value, such as muffled dialogue, sloppy edits, poor continuity, the committee will hit the stop button and move on to the next screener. I served as a juror for a major international festival, and trust me — there is more crap to navigate through than ever before in order to get to any well-made film that might have a shot against the competition, which is fierce.

With your really compelling script and the amount of time you put in to get it right, the workshops and the writing groups, you don't want inexperienced actors screwing it up. That would really be a waste of time and money. You want better actors to bring it to life. If you have an average story, or say, another teen-slasher been-there-seen-that picture, truly extraordinary actors can do wonders, increasing your chances of a distribution deal even if we've previously seen something similar. Rich, deep, vibrant, interesting acting is going to get you through better than anything else, unless you have crappy sound. Not much else is worse than poor sound quality — except poor acting. And now that anyone can make a movie, now more than ever, you need to learn just as much about the casting process as you do about filters, camera angles and digital sound recording.

Raise your standards.

It is imperative to surround yourself with people who know more than you do. It will raise you to a new skill level and make you a better artist. The world is full of egomaniacs who need to go home and get out of the way of those who have something real to contribute to the film industry. Please. Stop clogging up festival entry offices with crap.

All about editing.

After your great script and fantastic cast, it is all about the editor. Moving out of preproduction and getting on-set and into production is the result of months, perhaps years, of development. Once you are on-set, almost everything you do is for the benefit of the editor: all the charts and records, the log sheets, the continuity and getting through all the setups and reverse shots, and matched action. You work hard to get it right while you're shooting, because when it comes to reshoots and pick-ups, it's really challenging to reproduce exactly what you did six weeks ago. Everything we do on-set is so the movie will cut well in postproduction. Great editing feels seamless. Great editing is, ideally, easy to completely ignore because the audience's attention is captured by the story and the performances as it should be. This happens when you give the editor great footage to work with. The right actors in each role will make your days on-set a dream and your nights in the edit suite a breeze of beautiful choices that match — as in *action that matches* in scenes that cut together seamlessly.

Inexperience costs more money.

An inexperienced gaffer will take more time to get the lighting ready, which will lead to more and longer days. An inexperienced assistant director (AD) will drag down your day-to-day production scheduling. It's true in all aspects of your crew and actors. When you work with inexperienced actors, you will have fewer choices and you will have to do more takes. When you work with actors who can't match their action from one day to the next, you will have a tougher time editing. And the movie will suffer.

So why not get the best actors you can for your movie? Why not spend as much time thinking about casting as you do about filters and storyboards? You'd think this would be a given. Anyone about to embark on making a movie ought to know to spend time casting. Well, my friend, in more than 30 years in film and theatre, it amazes me what I've seen left behind, forgotten or never even considered.

The best actors are the right actors.

The right actors will bring your story to life and improve the chances of your movie making it into the festivals. The wrong actor in a role can tank your project before you ever get through the first setup on the first day. Make a list of great books that could have been great movies but for bad casting. Let's not forget Leslie Howard as Ashley Wilkes in *Gone With The Wind*, the ultimate Hollywood legend of bad casting. What was the difference between Tom Hanks in *The Da Vinci Code* and *Forrest Gump*? Why did the same actor, so brilliant as Forrest Gump, take such a critical hit with both Dan Brown books? Was he was simply miscast? It happens. A lot.

TECHNOLOGY HAS CHANGED EVERYTHING

Prescreening footage.

Technology has transformed the casting process and will save you money. It is now possible to prescreen actor submissions and greatly cut down on the number of actors to meet by appointment at a script reading. Any actor who has the chops — and you don't want to work with actors who don't — all have demo reels and websites with sample footage from their portfolios for you to prescreen. Anyone who submits to your project can now send you a footage file, or a link to his or her footage. Any actor who stalls on this point isn't taking his career seriously and you wouldn't want him anywhere near your production. He will waste your time, and time is money. By the way — how many days do you have on that camera rental?

The headshot submission process has gone green.
No more paper printed headshots! Very few actors mail printed headshots anymore. Truly, I can't remember the last time I got a submission notice for hard copies of headshots outside theatre productions where this remains the standard. The magic of electronic headshot submissions, actor websites and demo-footage submissions means you can sit on the beach with your laptop and a beer, or at home in a bathrobe sipping coffee, pre-screening hundreds of actors who are interested in auditioning for your film. It's also the sustainable way to go.

SAVING MONEY RECAP

You will save money because you...

- ...won't need to rent that P.O. Box to receive paper headshots.
- ...will be spending less on renting a rehearsal hall to run the auditions.
- ...will utilize technology to your advantage with electronic submissions and email correspondence.
- ...will save money on actor fees by finding unknown and up-and-coming new faces.
- ...will save money working with experienced actors by knowing contract specifics.
- ...will save money by doing many — and in some cases, *all* — of the casting procedures yourself.
- ...will save money by knowing when to bring in a casting director.
- ...will save money knowing you have actors who have the experience to get you through 12- to 14-hour days, including how to make their mark, match action, etc.
- ...will have a better chance at selling your movie, reimbursing your investors, and making money by landing a distribution deal if your movie is well-acted, well-crafted, with a compelling story audiences will enjoy.

CHAPTER TWO

YOUR DIRECTING CAREER

> "Pick up a camera. Shoot something. No matter how small, no matter how cheesy, no matter whether your friends and your sister star in it. Put your name on it as director. Now you're a director. Everything after that you're just negotiating your budget and your fee." — James Cameron

BETTER CASTING IMPACTS YOUR LONG-RANGE CAREER GOALS

Directing careers are built on leadership, vision and previous successes. As your projects gain more attention over time by winning festival awards and gaining good press coverage, you will work with known actors. Eventually you will need to learn how to work with agents and casting directors. For now, the do-it-yourself model is best for small projects. Work with actors, speak their language, and run professional casting sessions.

Actors want to work with the best directors regardless of the budget. If you've got a great script, actors are going to want to get onboard.

SHORTS CAN BE YOUR STEPPING STONE

Many directors start their careers with short films, submitting to the plethora of shorts festivals, from the 48-Hour Festival to shorts programs in major film festivals to online competitions. Some directors make a name for themselves first as actors, and then make the crossover because they now have the personal funds and industry connections to do so. George Clooney, Kevin Costner and Helen Hunt have all directed, among many others. The market is huge, with a lot of opportunity.

A great resource for finding shorts festivals is *withoutabox. com*, a division of *imdb.com* (The Internet Movie Database). While no one has quite figured out how to make much money on shorts, audiences love them. Festival organizers burn compilation DVDs with revenue usually remaining with the festival, not flowing back to the artist. (Carefully read the release agreement for each festival!) Short films can be a stepping stone to securing funding for a longer version of your story, especially if you're winning festival awards. Shorts can also be a proving ground for your working team: When it's time to move up to a feature, you will have confidence in your designers and key crew, prove to investors that you can deliver product, and achieve the return on investment. As you work with bigger budgets, you will be able to afford more known actors.

WHERE TO CONNECT WITH ACTORS

Networking with actors and learning to speak their language is going to help you become a better director. In the United States, actors live and work in cities where there is a vibrant theatre community: places like New York City, Chicago, Boston, Seattle, San Francisco and Portland, Oregon. Actors are drawn to cities with great theatre because for many actors, theatre is their first love due to the live aspect of the audience feedback. Many actors tend to do movies and television to support their low-paying theatre work. Actors often build credibility in theatre by gaining experience and dabbling a bit in local film projects before making the decision to move to Los Angeles to pursue television and movie acting.

Los Angeles has a lot of theater because when actors aren't on a movie or television set making money, they enjoy working in front of a live audience. For you, the early career director, it's time to start going to the theatre. While you're at it, check out the comedy clubs and the improvisational theatre groups in your community. If you are looking for an affordable unknown great comic actor, where else to look but in the comedy and improv clubs? These are the places agents look for new talent. It works for agents and talent managers. Why not you?

BREAKING BARRIERS:
HOW TO TALK TO ACTORS

Actors are not the insecure egomaniacs the media would like you to believe. They are also not "a dime a dozen." It's true there are many people flocking into auditions because they believe they can act. It's your job to distinguish between talent and ego, between artist and personality, between craft and crap. Hopefully you'll get better at sorting headshots and reviewing online footage, and you'll be able to audition only the best and brightest.

To better comprehend just what constitutes great acting, watch it live onstage, in the moment. Make it a new habit: go to the theatre. Build your own new appreciation for how actors do what they do.

The good actors are worth their weight in gold, and you'd be lucky to have the privilege of casting one in your movie. It all starts with respect. If you abuse actors, speak ill of them, treat them with the attitude that they aren't worth much, then that is what you're going to get at your auditions: the bottom of the barrel. It's time to recognize that without good actors, you may as well power down the lens and go home.

Blame the media.

Actors don't have more drug and alcohol related problems than any other demographic in the population. It's just that we hear about it more often because it makes the news reports. We don't hear about dejected and depressed plumbers. It's not newsworthy. But a box-office star is. When Mel Gibson is busted for driving under the influence, it's news. When Britney Spears is hospitalized, it's news. We worship celebrity, and when celebrities fall from grace, they fall hard, and the public loves to watch the drama. It doesn't mean that all actors are addicts. For the most part they are highly trained, have invested thousands of hours and dollars into their careers, and would love to just stay employed. They have mortgages to pay and children to raise just like you do. They just happen to enjoy creating characters and entertaining audiences. They became actors instead of painters or photographers. They prefer to create in collaborative groups, just like you do.

CHAPTER THREE

AN OVERVIEW OF THE CASTING PROCESS

"People are cast for very different reasons. Arnold Schwarzenegger is not an artist, but he has every right to be called an actor. Meryl Streep is an artist of the first order. Both require respect, but for different reasons. One, because she is a major artist, the other because he is a cultish, physical specimen seen in heroic proportion. Actors/artists often require the abilities of equally special people to see their potential. But most films and film castings are not based on an actor's artistic potential."
— J. MICHAEL MILLER, The Actors Center

"All the world's a stage and all the men and women merely players. They have their exits and their entrances, and one man in his time plays many parts... " — WILLIAM SHAKESPEARE, *As You Like It*

Directors Speak: In Session

ON MAKING ADJUSTMENTS:

❝ *I asked an actor to give me a very still, filmic version of the big bombastic speech he'd just delivered. He asked permission to sit across from me at my table and make eye contact with me, then he delivered the most sincere, connected, authentic speech I've ever seen in audition. I've never forgotten it. He made a huge adjustment in response to my direction. He got the leading role.* ❞

■ ■ ■ ■ ■

WHY CAST THIS PERSON?

❝ *Personality and reputation: They were open, warm and professional in person, usually with a good sense of humor. I felt they would be a pleasure to work with. They respected me, enjoyed my direction, knew something about me, and were interested in the project. When I checked with other directors who had worked with them, the response came back 100% positive: low-maintenance, reliable, a good team member, cooperative, creative, disciplined, a positive attitude, consistently friendly with the rest of the cast/crew/staff, no emotional baggage or moodiness, seemed pleased to be with us and freely supportive of the project.* ❞

One of my favorite things to do is to make the call and offer an actor a role. Actors hear "No" more than 90% of the time, so when they do land a job, it's a very happy day indeed.

Every movie made has its own timeline, from announcing the auditions to offering the roles and signing contracts. However, there are certain standards that we can learn from and common procedures and processes that make the process truly exciting and enjoyable.

WHAT ARE YOU CASTING:
Preliminary Considerations.

Evaluate your casting requirements. Your job is to filter actor submissions and find those who are "right" in regard to the required skill set, whether that is a real French accent or the ability to run hurdles on the track. If you need a stunt athlete, know that too.

Casting procedures vary according to the type of project and the market. Commercials tend to cast fairly quickly. If you're hiring one or two actors for a pharmaceutical spot, you need less time than you would for two leads and five supporting actors in a short or feature narrative film. If your commercial is airing nationally, you are going to look for actors who can carry a national audience, appealing to the broadest demographic in the advertising target audience. If your spot is a local used car lot, you are more likely looking for someone who appeals to your local market. If your leading actor is tall, you probably will be looking for tall supporting partners. If your script calls for someone who has a particular athletic skill, you need to put that specifically in the casting breakdown. For example, if you need someone who can do tricked-out skateboard moves, be sure the dude standing in front of you can deliver. Have the actor bring footage of himself doing the moves, or hold the audition at a skate park. If you have to have a redheaded woman, and the blonde is a better actor, remember the wonders of hair dye. You can change an actor's hair color. Changing ethnicity is more difficult. Express exactly the special skills and acting attributes required to shoot the job.

When it comes to industrial training films, you can screen for assorted special work environment skills, such as medical terminology or legalese vocabulary. If you're casting a commercial requiring someone to play a doctor, you can state specifically whether the actor must be a doctor. Advertising rules have changed, and hiring someone for, say, an arthritis medication advertisement, may now require that the actor actually have the ailment the pharmaceutical remedies. High blood pressure medication advertising, for instance, now requires that the spokesperson and actors in the spot have high blood pressure.

Families and lovers.

If you are creating the true look of a family, you need to consider physical attributes and externals — hair and eye coloring, facial bone structure, etc. You want plausible family relatives where there is blood relation. Look at the casting on *Meet The Fockers*, with Dustin Hoffman and Barbra Streisand. The actor playing their son, Ben Stiller, physically looks like someone this couple would produce. When there isn't blood, and it's an in-law, for example, you can go for extreme opposites with great results. Review the ensemble casting on the television series *Everybody Loves Raymond*, for one example.

Remember that old phrase "opposites attract"? Consider how well these romantic pairings worked: Helen Hunt and Jack Nicholson in *As Good As It Gets*; Halle Berry and Billy Bob Thornton in *Monster's Ball*; Maggie Gyllenhaal and Jeff Bridges in *Crazy Heart*.

A thorough casting breakdown is in order for your project to go any further. So get specific with everything. Gender, age range and ethnicity are the easy part. You've got to know what is in your script, and who these people are.

CASTING IS...

"Casting" is the term applied to the process of finding the best actors for roles in your movie, whether a short or a feature, for television or broadcast, theatrical distribution or film festival entry.

"Audition" is the term used to describe the job interview procedure used during the casting process. There are many kinds of auditions: open call, first-rounds, private appointments, callbacks, cold readings, etc., which are all part of the bigger picture of casting.

Casting breaks down into two major areas: principal and background casting. Let's look at each:

Principal casting.

Principal casting is all about who has lines and how many. Any character in your movie with lines will need to go through principal casting and have a reading with you, the director. You will want to see choices.

Principal casting is divided into "Lead" roles, "Supporting" roles, "Day Players" and "Under-Five." Lead roles are evident: the story revolves around your leads and they appear on screen the most. Supporting roles can be in every scene, on screen just as much as a lead, but the story isn't about them. They support the lead's story. Also, supporting roles can be anywhere from more than one day on-set, to every day on-set. A Day Player is just that: an actor on-set for one day only. You can film everything that character appears in on one day, usually just a few scenes, perhaps only one, and not a huge line load. And an Under-Five generally means under five lines and in one scene, and will only be needed half a day. Go through your script and identify each character to create your audition notice so actors know what kind of a role they are auditioning for. Actors appreciate knowing if they are auditioning for a major supporting role with multiple scenes and two weeks on-set, or a two-day role requiring only three days on-set.

Background casting.

Background casting is also known as extras casting. Extras do not speak. If an extra is given a line and is noticeable in a scene, it becomes an upgrade, and this person is no longer an extra. On union shoots, an upgrade is a bump in pay rate and must be noted. Sometimes non-union extras given an upgrade can become eligible for union standing if they have other union projects they've worked on.

If you need a lot of extras, assign someone on your staff to get this done, or contract with a background casting company. Background casting professionals are amazing at finding everyday people to fill the street scenes, the crowds, the stadium filled with cheering fans, the roadside rubbernecks at the scene of the crime, the police officers wandering around in the background.

When you get into big-budget Screen Actors Guild (SAG) projects, there will be a quota of how many union extras you need on-set to fulfill your contract. And the ratio varies. If you need 100 extras, then a percentage of them will need to be union and the rest can be non-union. These ratios vary according to the type of contract you are using. Non-union films have no quota, and no limits. Get the most up-to-date information from the SAG website (*sag.org*). Your local SAG office will negotiate exactly what the percentage has to be, which is determined by your budget and type of contract.

TYPES OF AUDITIONS

Open calls.

An "open call" audition is an advertised time and place where actors can show up without an appointment. Open calls are great when you need a lot of extras, or you are in a town in need of community support to embrace film production. Open calls can win the hearts of the community and generate "buzz," media coverage and other benefits to your marketing plan.

Open calls are also referred to as "cattle calls." The metaphor is fairly clear: herds of people standing in lines, waiting to see someone, wanting to work on your movie. Open calls don't have to be unpleasant, but when casting your leading and supporting roles, you can easily avoid them. Reality shows love open calls because it makes for great, cheap production filler and high ratings. Everyone will tune in with hopes of seeing themselves.

Appointments: script readings, cold readings and improvisation.

A scheduled appointment is the preferred way of meeting an actor for the first time. When you are serious about reading actors for a specific role, you are ready to take the time to schedule appointments and not have people standing around waiting to see you. Be more respectful of people's time. An appointment audition is a meeting with an actor who is a true potential for your project. They appear right for the role based on their headshot, resume and reel submissions, which you have already reviewed. You like their "look" and want to hear them read a scene. So you have contacted them, or their agent, and set up an appointment to come in. They have the appropriate experience for either a lead or a supporting role.

When actors have scripts ahead of time for an appointment with you, it's called a "script reading." When actors have had very little time to prepare or are looking at a script for the first time standing there in front of you, it's called a "cold reading." Try to avoid cold readings. Everyone deserves to prepare.

Another type of appointment audition includes the use of improvisation. This is a great tool in the audition process to test spontaneity and confidence. You will quickly see whether the actor takes risks and is comfortable in the spotlight. When casting comedy, ask to have them bring a few jokes, or a trick, or something comedic. You need to know if they can deliver a punchline. For physical comedy, have them show you something in their box of "tricks" — a pratfall, juggling, etc. Set up scenes similar to the given circumstances in your story and let the actors make up the lines. See what happens! You'll find improvisation allows some actors to relax in the work, rather than working off a script they've had no time to study or prepare. Try to remember that some actors are terrible at improvisation and prefer to prepare scripted material. You will want to avoid dropping someone from your possibilities if they were great at script reading and terrible at improvisation.

When it comes time to scheduling your background extras, there is no need for appointments. This is the time to have an open call.

Callbacks.

A "callback" is the next logical step after your initial round of first-time meetings. There may be several rounds of callbacks until your mind is made up. Actors understand callbacks are necessary and expect it to take time. It's not unusual to audition for projects with four or more callback rounds. It's part of the business.

I have auditioned for parts that took three or four callbacks and still didn't get the role. One time on a television movie project, I was the second choice for a great supporting role, and they were waiting to see if an up-and-coming new actor on the scene was going to accept the role. She did. It was an honor to know I was in consideration against her (years later she would win the Academy Award). They really liked me, and I was happy with the minor role they did give me. I had a great time working with a very well-known "A-list" actor that day who was also the producer. Also, I've cast projects where we started over with first-time appointments after the callbacks yielded only the desire to keep looking.

At the callback you are going to read additional scenes from the script (more on this in Chapter Ten). Once you have your lead actor, you will bring in the candidates for the supporting roles, one at a time, to read with your lead, looking for the right match. Callbacks are exciting and you will look forward to hearing the script read well by experienced actors who will bring it to life.

Now that you understand open calls, appointment auditions and callbacks, there are a few standards to mention right away:

CASTING STANDARDS

Above all, keep it professional.

Keeping things professional means keeping things confidential. No one is rejected because they "suck." You must learn to be kind. Actors don't get a role because they *weren't what you were looking for,* or *they just weren't what the director had in mind.* Practice these simple phrases and leave it at that. Let the agents do their job of improving their client's callback ratio and landing a job. If any actor truly "sucks" at auditioning, they won't be getting much attention from agents because they won't be booking jobs. So get used to it: You will have to learn to keep all discussions related to casting completely confidential. You will need to have a staff that respects and understands why casting discussions are kept private. You will find yourself evaluating in intimate detail why you prefer one actor over another, and you need to trust your staff to follow professional standards and protocol. You need to be ready to fire those who violate confidence.

Directors and producers must be free to discuss the merits of one actor over another without reprisal. For one thing, there are libel suits. You do not ever want the reasons you chose one actor over another to circulate on a social networking site posted by an inexperienced crewmember. If you're working with people you don't know well, think about getting it in writing. Have your producers and anyone else in on casting sessions sign a confidentiality agreement. Protect yourself from those who can't keep quiet. These decisions can make or break your movie.

Never settle.

When in doubt, keep looking: There are plenty of fish in the sea. There's a plethora of wonderful actors just waiting to hear about your project, who want to work, who are trained to work, who are perfect for the role, if you could just find them. Always continue to search for the actor who is 100% perfect for the part.

Actors are looking for you as well.

Actors are trawling casting websites every day looking for new projects. Los Angeles and New York City actors working regularly in television are looking for great projects to do between seasons of their shows. There is no reason why your film can't be one of their summer projects.

Agents are looking for projects for their clients.

It is possible to get through to agents. They want good scripts for their clients. That is why they are in business. A client may bring a script to their agent's attention after finding a good role posted online.

A great script will open doors.

The entire industry is thirsty for a refreshing new idea, on the edge of their seats for the next really great must-see film. The opposite is also true. Don't submit your script to an agency if it hasn't been thoroughly proofed, reviewed, improved upon and is in excellent shape artistically as well as commercially. Agents want to know your film is going to get made and do something wonderful for their client.

Casting centers in the U.S. are
New York City and Los Angeles.

When it is time to plan your fishing trip, go to the biggest lakes. For casting, that's Los Angeles and New York City. That is not to say you won't find perfect actors in your own city. Almost any city with a vibrant film and theatre arts community is going to have great actors.

It's a job interview.

Keep in mind that auditions are job interviews. You want to find out more about this person — whom, based on their submission materials, you think is right for the role. Can you communicate your ideas to this actor? Do they have the level of experience needed for the size of the role? Do they have stamina, patience and sense of humor to hold up for 12 or 14 hours of shooting? Do they understand the script? Do they "get" the story? Do they "get" you?

CASTING IS NOT...

Casting is not about you; it's about making a great film. Casting is not about having hordes of gorgeous young men and women parading past you seeking approval. While it may feel good, it's a waste of time.

Casting is not a party.

Keep your casting sessions professional, polite, respectful, and on time. Consider yourself warned: You're going to be asked by all your friends if they can audition for you. Get used to saying "No." No one has time for gratuitous auditions. You must keep things moving along and audition only those experienced performers who are right for a role. That might include your best friend, your neighbor and your babysitter — but only if they are absolutely right for the role. It's fun to work with our friends, and we all like to be surrounded by people who really like us. Moviemaking is hard work.

What's the big deal? Why not have your friends in the leading roles? Because when the rubber meets the road, are you going to be able to fire your best friend when they don't know their lines? Will you still love them tomorrow? You're going to want your best friend next to you when the theater goes dark. You're going to want your best friend there after 14 hours of shooting when you want to hang your gaffer out to dry for not giving you what you wanted. You're going to want your best friend to stand by you no matter what. Keep your friends. Casting is not about making friends, although you will make lasting friendships and work with the same people again. Casting is about the movie. Keep that foremost in your mind. Be certain that this is the right person for the job, or keep looking. If your friend truly is the best choice for the role, go for it. Be certain they always tell the truth, and won't get mad or walk off the set.

Casting is not about your ego: Get over yourself.
Casting is about finding the perfect actor for the role. Don't call people in to audition for a favor. Don't call people who might be right for something. Only call people in who are completely right, who fit the character type, whose work you like, who you can communicate with, who can create the person you see in your head.

TO UNION OR NOT

Thoroughly evaluate your decision.
If you are in this for the long haul, and plan to make movies for the rest of your life, you will have to learn to handle union contracts and the preproduction paperwork necessary to become a union-approved project. You hope to someday work

with known actors, and most television and film actors are members of the performers' unions. You may as well jump in and learn the ropes. Stand by, roll camera:

Let us agree your story is good to great with high production values, leading to a sense of confidence about getting into festivals. Your team has other feature and festival credits and you are looking at the budget wondering if you can afford union actors. You may perceive that it's complicated and expensive to go union. You may already have someone in mind, having reached his or her agent and submitted your script. Perhaps this actor with a marketable name has said "Yes" to your script. A marketable name means the actor has a body of work — films that have played festivals and have national and international distribution. It is likely this hypothetical actor is a union member.

Professional actors belong to these unions: (You may also find performers who are also members of the various musicians' unions.)

✓ AEA — Actors Equity Association; covers stage productions, Broadway, big touring productions of Broadway plays and musicals, regional repertory theatres and, in some cases, casino shows;

✓ AFTRA — American Federation of Television and Radio Artists; covers game shows, daytime dramas, broadcast news, television commercials, corporate industrials, radio, some primetime television;

✓ SAG — Screen Actors Guild; covers television movies, feature films, some television shows.

Before the digital revolution, which union had jurisdiction over a project was determined by whether you were shooting film (super 8mm, 16mm, 35mm, 70mm) or a three-camera videotaped studio shoot such as a sitcom with a live audience, and where you're project was headed: theatrical release or television. So if a television movie of the week was shot on film on location, it fell under a SAG contract. A three-camera "live to tape" studio television shoot, however, was done under an AFTRA contract. Camera technology has changed all that. Now new distribution venues, direct video sales and marketing are reshaping jurisdiction even more.

One member makes a union shoot.

If your prospective leading actor is a member of AFTRA or SAG, you will need to arrange a union contract. You will still be able to put a non-union actor in a role on a union shoot provided they are not a "must join." This means they have already worked on union film sets and are no longer eligible to work as a non-union actor. They are a "must join" — as in "must join" the union to work.

On the flip side, if your production's cast of characters is limited, and it's not essential that anyone in the cast have a marketable name, you may decide to work non-union. Once you hire union actors, however, you will need to follow the union contract and honor your obligations. If your budget cannot afford the day rates and you do have a union actor willing to say "Yes," and you want that actor in the role, there are options. SAG has a deferred pay contract among others. Many union actors will say "No" to deferred pay. You will have to look at other contracts available to you, including Low-budget, Ultra Low-budget, Limited Exhibition, Experimental, Student, etc.

In general, union actors tend to have more experience. Remember this when casting a leading role. Avoid considering actors without sufficient experience for a supporting role or lead. Experienced actors know how to shoot a scene. They know angles and frame lines, and how to match action. They know how to prepare a lead character and what to play on page 78, shooting on the first day, and page 34, shooting on day 20. This is not to say you won't find great non-union actors out there. Remember that when you use inexperienced actors it will take more time. Very experienced directors have the communication skills to work with new talent, how to coax better performances out of actors, how to direct them. If you don't have a lot of experience with actors, extend your shooting schedule. Be patient. You will get better at it.

Experience gets more done.

In general, the shorter the shooting schedule, the more experience everyone needs. Let's break it down: If you've got 18 days on your camera rental and a decent day rate for your director of photography (DP), you're looking at shooting five pages a day for the entire time on a 90-page feature, a schedule leaving very little wiggle room for any drop in the pace. It'll keep your 1st and 2nd assistant directors (ADs) very busy and on the ball.

The less experience, the longer your day.

Expect more takes of each setup when working with inexperienced actors. Double-check your actor's marks, frame line and matching action. When working non-union, schedule more time to get things done.

Questions for homework.

Seriously look at your budget, goals and priorities before coming to a decision on whether to go union or non-union. Discuss these questions with your producers and do the best you can to make the right decision for your production.

Can you get the return on your investment without a name actor in the lead? Do you have a longer shooting schedule to accommodate less experienced actors?

Do you have enough experience to work with union actors?

Are you confident with your communication skills regarding how to talk to actors to get the results you want?

How large is your cast?

What is your expectation for distribution after a film festival?

What is your true budget?

In any case, check reels and their other film performances. Hiring the wrong actor will ruin your project. Hiring an inexperienced actor for a leading role can kill your project. The perfect actor physically may not have the chops yet for a lead and would be better off in a supporting role while they gain more experience. As in any employment environment, check references and get feedback from other directors who have worked with this actor. You don't want just another pretty face; you want performances that really make a difference. You want a professional.

WHEN TO START

When actors read a casting breakdown, three things jump out: Is there a character that fits their particular demographic? When is it scheduled? What does it pay? Some actors only submit to projects that pay, that offer a role they are perfect for, or are shooting when they are available. Some actors will and some won't work for what your budget can afford. Some actors submit to everything out there regardless of suitability, and you'll just have to filter out the ones who don't match your demographics. We wish they wouldn't, as it is time-consuming to weed them out. It is just part of your sorting process.

Plan ahead to stay ahead.

Timing is everything — whether to shoot next summer or next spring, when to repeat the theme song, when to release your picture, when to start casting. The right time to start casting for actors is while you're writing or reading the script. As you read, visualize who you see in a role. You may have written the script for a particular actor, and you'll need to get on their production schedule two or five years from now. The only wrong time to start is too late to get it all done before you shoot.

How much time you need depends on the size of your cast — how many leads, how many supporting roles, how many days with more than 30 extras. The more actors you need, the longer it takes to get through all the submissions, schedule the auditions, do callbacks, do another round of callbacks, offer contracts, get the counter-offers, and then find yourself starting over because the lead actor you wanted is no longer available.

For most low-budget feature films with less than 10 major speaking roles, three months prior to your first shoot day is most likely going to give you the time you need to prepare and line up the actors you really want, provided that you're not competing with a particular actor's television series schedule. Apart from the weather, one reason feature films are shot from May to September is because television series have ended for the season and actors are available, itching to go somewhere fun for the summer and shoot a feature. Actors want out of New York City and Los Angeles.

The best time to cast for next summer is during the late winter to early spring. If you're shooting a winter setting, then cast during the previous late summer and fall. Actors need advance notice to get your project on their schedules. While there are plenty of fish in the sea, the busiest actors are busy because they're good and they get a lot of offers. You will have to be patient and work around other production schedules.

At times you will have to scramble and find someone else for a role because the guy you thought you had just got a better paying offer. If your offer is the lead and the other one is a supporting role, who gets to book (contract) that actor for that time period will depend on many factors. Ultimately it is up to the actor, but be warned: Agents are going to go for the money, and advise their clients likewise.

Your script will need to be beyond good: It must be excellent. Your business skills and communication skills need to match up, or you'll be the director stuck with the next best thing.

WHAT YOU NEED TO START

You need a script.

Many projects are under script revisions throughout the entire shoot, so your casting script doesn't have to be your absolute final script. However, actors will be hesitant to jump onboard without reading the script prior to callbacks. This seems like an obvious thing that doesn't need to be discussed. However, on one feature, when there was no script to read before scheduling callbacks, a few actors declined to come in, which was too bad, because these actors had great film and television credits and were willing to work on a low budget. In the end, it's the film that lost because the director had fewer options for those roles and lost out on seeing some terrific talent that had already made it through rounds of prescreening headshots, resumes and reels.

Some actors get really nervous when there isn't a script available. They are willing to come to the first round of auditions, but only after reading it. They get suspicious that the director is flaky.

It's a red flag. Don't get caught flying it. Be sure your script is available.

You need "sides."

Script "sides" are scene cuttings given to actors to prepare before the audition. (See Chapter Eight for recommendations on workflow and files.) Typically, only sides are provided prior to auditions. Then the entire script is sent only to those actors who are called back. You protect your script by making it available only to those who are your top few choices for your leading and major supporting roles. There are story thieves everywhere. Protect your property.

Know the window of time you plan to shoot.

Actors need to know if you are shooting in June or January in Denver or Phoenix. Generally speaking, this means you will need your locations fully determined. This will affect whether a Denver SAG actor is hired as a "Local Hires Only" in Denver, or if that Denver actor needs to travel to Phoenix, and how. In this case you'll be paying a *"per diem"* (a daily allowance toward living costs) and travel expenses. Include the approximate shooting dates on your casting breakdown in order to attract actors to the project. Actors only can submit to projects when they know they have that time slot open to take on a project.

You're going to need a place to hold your auditions.

There will be much more to say on this topic in Chapter Six.

You need your SAG paperwork done.

You, or your producer, need to get paperwork into the SAG office long before you can advertise your casting breakdown. The SAG office needs your Limited Liability Corporation (LLC) completed before your SAG status is approved. You will also need your SAG signatory in place. These are the folks who put your budget into escrow and cut the checks to make payroll with all the deductions. You're going to need to have production liability insurance. You will need to provide SAG with a copy of your budget to determine which kind of contract you qualify for. And if you need permits, and who doesn't, you'll be filing these forms as well.

Welcome to the real world. All these forms must be completed before you begin looking for professional actors. You cannot make contract offers with shooting dates until all this is done. It is in your best interest to go to the SAG website (*sag.org*) and read the various types of actor contracts available. There are contracts where you pay very little per day based on your overall budget (Ultra Low-budget). There's even a contract where you don't pay a thing until you get a distribution deal (Deferred). Speak to the SAG representative. They will make every effort to help you. Find out what you need to do ahead of time. Professional actors are not going to sign on to your project without SAG approval. The industry standard websites, where the actors will find you, won't post your breakdown for a union shoot without your SAG status approved, and this means your signatory is in place. These are the checks and balances that keep it real.

Even if you find unions distasteful, and a lot of folks do, or even if you've sworn you'd never work with SAG again because of a bad experience and decide to go non-union on your next project, you still need plenty of time to prepare and get organized. Most of us look at the pile of paperwork and freak out. It's a lot. But think of it this way: Making a movie is easy. Any fool can make a movie. Making a great movie is hard and very few succeed.

Reality check.

Here's a buck, get a java. Make it a double espresso. The SAG paperwork is nothing compared to the legalese of a distribution deal, and you stand a better chance of landing one of these when your budget is clean, clear, and your SAG approval, LLC and insurance are legitimate. Do it right, straight out of the gate.

Chapter Four will go into specifics about casting timelines, and how much time to allow each person on the schedule. For now, get used to the idea of planning casting months in advance.

CHAPTER FOUR

INDUSTRY STANDARDS

> "Fasten your seatbelts, it's going to be a bumpy night."
> — BETTE DAVIS AS MARGO CHANNING, *All About Eve*

THE STANDARDS

The standard marketing package to expect from actors submitting to your audition breakdown includes: a headshot and resume, and either a link to online footage at one of the online websites set up for actor profiles, or a brief, email-attached video clip. You can specify your preference and specifics in the audition breakdown. Let's examine each of these elements:

ACTOR MARKETING MATERIALS

Headshots

In response to your audition announcement, you will receive a photo file attached to email. The headshot should open up to an 8" x 10" color photo of the head and shoulders, cropped for details of the face with the eyes clearly center, and the name on the front. It should be well lit, in focus, and cause an immediately positive response in you. The casting type, age range and style of an actor should jump off the page and either clearly say to you "Yes" or "No."

What makes a good headshot?

Good actors take classes on how to get the right headshot and find a good photographer who understands the particular necessities of headshot photography. Good actors avoid overly artistic or modeling shots. Actors avoid distracting jewelry and heavy makeup. Most important is that the headshot truly represent the actor's appearance, and not what they look like under special lighting conditions. When the person walks through the door, you should recognize them from their headshot. Anyone coming to an audition should know to have a headshot with their resume attached. Have your audition assistant bring a stapler, as many times actors forget to attach the resume.

Let us review these samples of professional headshots. We have four women and three men of varying ages, casting types and ethnicities. For the purposes of this book, these headshot samples are reproduced in black and white. Standard industry headshots are in color.

Photo credit: Stuart Locklear

Headshot samples.

Kari Wishingrad works in features, commercials and industrials in the San Francisco Bay Area. As you can see, she has a warm personality, is somewhere over 40, and has a terrific smile. The long curly hair says she's fun and confident. The eye contact exudes great communication skills. Kari plays a variety of comedic and dramatic roles as businesswomen, artists, teachers and moms. She is represented by Stars The Agency.

Photo Credit: Bradley K. Ross, playboxstudios.com

Above we see Stephanie Carwin, based in Los Angeles and San Francisco. In this shot she is going for leading-lady romantic roles, emphasizing her feminine beauty. Her personality, age-range and character type come bouncing off the page. Stephanie is represented by Kolstein Talent and Tonry Talent.

Photo Credit: Bradley K. Ross, playboxstudios.com

Depending on the role, actors will submit various versions of a headshot. Here is Stephanie again, understating the sensuality and going instead for the best friend or mom role. Note the differences in lighting, wardrobe, makeup, composition and how it affects your interpretation of what roles would be suitable for this actress.

On the next page we see a mid-to-late-30s to mid-40s Latina who plays career women, moms, best friends, lawyers and artists. Mary Garcia is a New York-based actress who has appeared on the daytime dramas *All My Children* and *One Life to Live*. She was featured in the Indie horror film *Hell Time Stories Anthology.* Her warm personality is evident.

Mary Garcia

Photo credit: Matt Karas, mattkaras.com

Shawn-Caulin Young is a classically good-looking young male. His character type is young leading man, best friend, artist-rebel, creative type, with a deep personality and sensitive presence. I can easily see him playing an artist in a 19th century period drama, or skateboarding around Venice Beach

Photo credit: Michael D'Ambrosia　　　　　　　　Shawn-Caulin Young

working his guitar. This headshot is a good example of a strong vertical emphasis layout.

His confidence is clear in this headshot and his resume backs up his experience. I see he is a union actor with strong television credits. His age range is early/mid-20s to mid-30s young adult. Shawn-Caulin lives in Los Angeles, and is managed by Tina Treadwell.

Next is an example of horizontal emphasis, which actors use to reflect film's aspect ratio. André Mathieu plays middle-aged dads, businessmen and high school coaches with great personality. That friendly smile is genuine. He would also make a great uncle, mentor, teacher or senator.

André Mathieu

Photo Credit: Rod Goodman

Another example of horizontal emphasis. Notice the difference between full-frame horizontal and one that is sized to fit a vertical aspect ratio. André is represented by Tonry Talent in San Francisco.

Andre Mathieu

Photo Credit: Jim Johnson

Fred Pitts

Photo credit: Stewart Locklear

When not on-set, Dr. Fred Pitts is an emergency room physician in San Francisco. A friendly face, early middle-aged, with very kind eyes, Fred is a great romantic leading man with a deep soul. This versatile actor has numerous credits and is represented in San Francisco by JE Talent.

Maxine Greco works the Texas and Louisiana markets on commercials, industrials, and independent features. She is bilingual and very marketable, playing middle-aged and up as young grandmothers and feisty women of all sorts. She is tough, yet vulnerable. Maxine is represented by The Atherton Group.

Maxine's headshot design uses a horizontal aspect ratio on a vertical emphasis headshot. Compare how this affects your response with the other horizontal headshots. Also, notice how Maxine has chosen not only an interesting font for her name, but one that functions more like a logo. This supports branding, and you will find it repeats on her business card and her

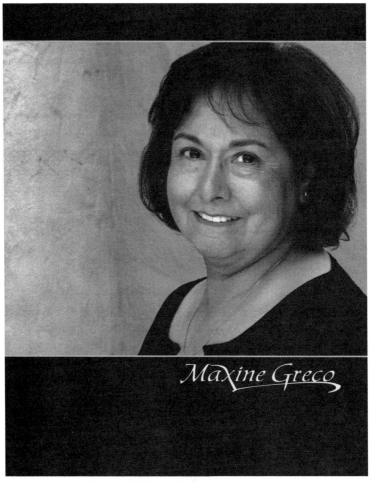

Photo credit: Chadd Green, PrimaDonna Productions, Inc. primadonnaproductions.com

website. It tells me she understands how important marketing, branding and name association are. It helps her to stand out.

What these headshots have in common is they are all about the face and the energy of the person depicted. The photographs are not about the lighting, or motion, or fashion. Notice how we gravitate to the eyes and get a sense of their personalities. We can easily place their ages, and we know what kind of roles they are best suited for. It's important to pay attention to how you respond to headshots.

Common mistakes early-career actors make with head-shots include inappropriate composition and poor cropping, too much makeup, fashion posing, shots that are out of focus, poor lighting, shots where the face and eyes don't "pop" off the page. Quite often young women playing the ingénue roles reveal too much skin, apply too much makeup and end up looking like they're ready for the porn industry.

"Camera-ready" actors with experience will always have an industry standard headshot done by professional photographers. It is, after all, the most important marketing tool that will either inspire you to click on a website to view their footage or not. Evaluating actors' headshots is another way to evaluate preparedness. When a professional isn't using the best marketing materials available, question it. Where else are they lacking? They may look perfect for the role, and looks can be deceiving.

You may also be given what is called a ¾ body shot and is typically head to thigh, giving you a better idea of body type. The 8" x 10" color headshot still remains the standard.

Resumes.

Resume formatting is shown here in the industry-standard three-column format, with the actor's name top center in a large and expressive font reflective of their personality. Font choice is another way actors can communicate something about themselves. Just below the name line, also center, are any union affiliations. Actors will list AEA (Actors Equity Association, Stage), SAG (Screen Actors Guild, Film), or AFTRA (American Federation of Television and Radio Artists) and occasionally music unions. You will also see "SAG eligible." Don't be confused between "must join," which may also be listed here, and "SAG eligible." Everyone is SAG *eligible*. The performer may be trying to get your attention to make you believe they have more experience than they do. If a performer meets the qualifications to join, they join. Membership is an honor as it validates readiness to work. "Must join" means just that: The next offer of a union contract will require joining; they have worked the required number of days on-set under a union contract, and simply can't do that anymore. Someone who is a "must join" can no longer work on a union contract as a non-union performer. Many actors hold off on joining for many reasons. It's expensive for one. The initiation fees can be more than a thousand dollars depending on the regional market.

Contact information is in the upper right corner and physical statistics are in the upper left. When reviewing information on a resume, look for any directors you might know, or the larger, more-known production companies. Remember, you are looking for common ground, experience, familiarity and anyone who could be a reference. Anyone with a lead in a feature you've never heard of can be verified on *imdb.com* (The Internet Movie Database).

You will at some point audition performers who have very little experience. The resume has a few classes listed; maybe a few short projects or student projects. That may be wonderful and ready and perfect. It's still a good idea to call their teacher, call the director or school and do a reference check. Expect professional actors to use the standards.

Three-column actor's resume template:

YOUR NAME

(Large and in an interesting font that adds personality.)

height   any union affiliations go under name   CELL PHONE
weight   PAGER
coloring   Email address
age range   (NEVER put home addresses on a resume)   Web Site

FILMS: (bolded)

Title of Film	Size of Role	Director/production company
Title of Film	Co-star/Supporting	Director/production company
Title of Film	principal	Director/production company
Title of Film	lead	Director/production company
Title of Film	under 5	Director/production company

TELEVISION:

Title of Show	Host	Director/Television Station
Title of Show	Featured	Director/Television Station
Title of Show	Co-host	Director/Television Station
Title of Show	Guest star	Director/Television Station

COMMERCIAL/INDUSTRIAL: (conflicts upon request, only if applicable)

product	Role	Distribution
Safeway Supermarkets	Radio Voice over	Regional/CBS, ABC, Cable
Bank of America	Co-star	In-House Training Film

THEATRE:

Title of play	Name of Character	Theatre Company/Director
Title of play	Name of Character	Theatre Company/Director
Title of play	Name of Character	Theatre Company/Director
Title of play	Name of Character	Theatre Company/Director

TRAINING:

Title of class	Name of Instructor	Studio or school
Actors Retreat	Hester Schell,	
	Robert Pickett	STUDIO SCHELL
Acting for the Camera	Hester Schell	Notre Dame De Namur University
Higher Education Degree	What degree	where

SPECIAL SKILLS: This is where you shine and show a sense of humor. You list anything and
everything that helps you stand out in a crowd. Juggling, dog racing, whatever you've got,
skateboarding, bass-baritone, sight-read music, American sign-language, fluent in Mandarin
and Spanish, certified sharp shooter, gun license,stick shift, stilt walking, rock climbing.
Don't just say sports. List them out. What about your day job? Chances are that it has medical
terminologyg, or legalese that would come in handy for industrials, etc. In today's market, if you
to work in action films, you need martial arts, weightlifting, weapon handling, stage combat. List
any stunt training above in TRAINING. If you've been a lawyer or a VP at a corporation, what are the
transferable skills. If you are a parent, what translates? List the ages of your children. Etc. etc .

Notice the text box is 8" x 10" so it will fit exactly on the back of your headshot. If your headshot is
currently 8.5" x 11" then you need to have it re-sized. The big time requires the industry standard.

Trim your edges
Attach resume to headshots
Never hand in untrimmed loose pages, never
expect the CD to do your secretarial work

Reels.

Demo reels are capsules of a person's work. It is a short commercial selling an actor's abilities on screen. Demo reels are typically under two or three minutes, and are front-loaded: the first 10 to 15 seconds are packed with a series of close-ups. By the end of this opener, you know what they look like in close-up, and the quality of their voices. The reel will then move on to longer scene edits that focus on the actor, not on the scene partner. Do not expect entire scenes or trailers. A well-edited demo reel will have clear sound with professional-level production values. The reel will open easily in a standard movie player such as QuickTime. It will not be in some unknown format that only opens on an iPhone. Footage submissions must be generic so they can open on any computer.

WHY LOOK FOR THE STANDARDS?

When you are reviewing hundreds of headshots, you will learn to appreciate that the contact information is always in the upper right hand corner, so it is easily accessible. You will learn to recognize a good headshot and high-quality demo footage. You will see that professionals have professional marketing materials — a clear indication of whether they are ready to be on your movie set. An actor who doesn't know the industry standards may be lacking the on-set experience you need to get through your long days. An actor who knows the industry standards is ready to work.

You will get variations on the headshot resume standards. Be forgiving when you get a preformatted photo and resume from an online database where you've posted your announcement and will be reviewing submissions. Every database has a different layout. The Internet has changed even the 8" x 10" photo standards.

On a feature I cast in 2009, several thousand actors submitted for seven supporting roles that paid $100 a day on a

SAG Ultra Low-budget contract. That's right: several thousand. People want to work. Union actors must work a certain number of days to maintain health coverage. So they apply to everything possible.

I was able to sort out those who had experience *and* were right for the role fairly quickly by reviewing online reels. We were able to schedule less than 50 actors for these seven roles and found a great cast, ready to work. Because of industry standards I was able to efficiently get from thousands to less than a hundred, then down to those we wanted to meet. Through the final sorting process our leading man, a known actor, chose who he wanted to meet. As a result we narrowed choices down to five or six excellent actors for each role. We did a nationwide search on the websites suggested in this book. Industry standards work. Why work substandard?

Step up to the plate. The banquet is before you. With your fantastic story, well-crafted script and a budget, you can utilize industry standards to reach actors and agents, make submissions, schedule auditions with the best actors available. Agents and actors are out there looking for projects right now. They will be looking on the industry standard websites where you will place your posting. Good luck and we all hope to see your film at a festival.

CHAPTER FIVE

ACTING — WHAT IS IT?

"If I feel the part is right, and I know that the producers and the director want me, I'd go for broke. Always."
— ANNE ARCHER, Actress

"Acting is by far and away the toughest job, in terms of filmmaking and maybe even the arts. How they do it I don't know, but they have to be allowed to get their satisfaction." — JONATHAN DEMME

Actors Speak: In Session

❝ *As I waited to read, I overheard the casting director on the phone making a deal for another actor to get the role I was reading for. When he called me in to read, he never even looked at me, rushed me and said 'thank you and goodbye.' They totally wasted my time.* **❞**

■ ■ ■ ■ ■

❝ *I was asked if I wouldn't mind driving 12 hours to audition at a secret location in Vermont. It was an intimate scene with two award-winning 'A-list' actors. I did it. I got a call three days later to hold the date, and was told, 'Director loved the tape.' They even gave me a phone number. After patiently waiting two weeks I used the number only to find it was disconnected. They had abruptly closed shop and moved the location back to Hollywood without informing anyone. Just let people know what's going on. We just want to know what's going on.* **❞**

One afternoon in the summer of 1999, while working on a feature along the San Mateo County coastline in California, a thin, quirky young woman stopped by our set to visit her husband, who was starring in the film we were so busy with. I wondered if her exuberance had something to do with her husband and his pending day off. She was terribly excited about this independent film she'd been working on. She chatted on about the director and how she thought the film might turn out "okay" and maybe get into a few festivals. The young woman I met that day had just wrapped the lead on *Boys Don't Cry*. In a few months she would win the Academy Award.

Great acting is transformative; it is the action, guts and backbone of your story. It is how your plot travels through time, moment by moment, action and reaction by action and reaction. When acting is great, it completely transports you to another time in another place, and, like ballet, looks effortless. When you have the right actor in the right role, your entire film will simply take off, as it did for Hilary Swank in *Boys Don't Cry*. Her breathtaking performance catapulted her to stardom. When I sat in the theatre after the credit roll of *Brokeback Mountain*, I had that same sense of total awe and wonder. You just never know exactly how an actor and a role will meet and make magic. When actors get it right, they really get it right.

Great acting on stage in front of a live audience is entirely different than great acting in a movie. Each has its particular elements of craft, with differing approaches and ways of preparation from the actor's point of view. Whether casting for film or theatre, from the director's point of view, it's the same: Find the best actor for the role. In casting, it's your job to see everyone you can possibly see for each role to find the absolute perfect match.

Like the court justice who defined porn — "I know it when I see it" — great acting is about how you respond to an actor playing a character in a story. It's different for each of us. We all have our favorites. Who you like is who you like. There are the legends we tend to agree on: Meryl Streep, Dustin Hoffman, Heath Ledger. We know of actors who sink themselves so far into a role that it leaves us gasping for air; actors who have that magical ability to completely transform from role to role. There are character actors and sex symbols, and there are the passing fancies, the pop star performers who come and go from drug rehab to stay in the news. Then there are the gods and goddesses of the silver screen: no matter what they're starring in, we go to their movies. And we go by the millions. It drives huge international business, feeds the economy, provides jobs, feeds families, sustains communities. Our industry is Big Business.

There are performances we will never forget. My list includes: Meryl Streep in *The French Lieutenant's Woman* and *Angels In America*; Ralph Fiennes in *The English Patient*; Elizabeth Taylor in *Cat On a Hot Tin Roof*; Dustin Hoffman in *Little Big Man, Rain Man* or *The Graduate*; Hilary Swank in *Boys Don't Cry*; Heath Ledger in *Brokeback Mountain*; Vivien Leigh in *Gone With The Wind*; Jimmy Stewart in *The Philadelphia Story*; Cary Grant in *The Philadelphia Story*; Katharine Hepburn in *The Philadelphia Story*. It's difficult to imagine anyone else in these roles. We call this the "perfect match" of actor to role.

When an entire ensemble soars into awards season, as have the entire casts of Masterpiece Theatre's *Bleak House*, television series such as *ER, Friends, Frasier, Everybody Loves Raymond, Cheers* and *Seinfeld*, or Indie hits like *The Hangover*, we call this perfect casting. Consider the casting on *The Philadelphia Story, The Big Lebowski, Crash*. Every actor fits every role perfectly. The casting process got it right, from the leads to every bit player, and it shows.

Acting defined.

Every acting teacher you talk to is going to give you a varying definition of what acting is and how an actor does what she does. While there are varying approaches and concepts, we tend to agree that acting is creating a character within a story for the benefit of the audience.

The actor's toolbox.

Actors have a toolbox, just like your art director or your gaffer has a toolbox. The actor's toolbox basically consists of three things: the voice and the body and how they use the immediate space around them. The voice can be manipulated through diction, placement, volume, accents, dialects, rhythm, impediments, phrasing, pausing, breathing, and so on. The body changes through stillness or movement, how weight is carried, whether costumed for period or contemporary, etc. The space around an actor can be the entire stage or the frame line.

Script Analysis: If it ain't on the page, it ain't on the stage.

Professional actors do script analysis. Anyone who thinks they can just phone in a great performance, matching action and continuity of performance without adequate preparation, is a phony. Good actors analyze scripts searching for clues as to how to play the character. They look at transitions between scenes, and complications, and how the plot and action work on character. They look for how other characters describe them, and how they describe themselves. They look at the things they do: the actions, and the consequences of these actions. All these choices an actor makes with voice and body find a reason in the script. For example, any actor anywhere about to play Brick in *Cat On a Hot Tin Roof* is going to play an alcoholic man with a broken foot in a cast who uses a crutch. Choices come from the text and must be justified by the text. One directing teacher, Larry Arrick, taught me I could do anything to a script that I wanted, only if I could justify it in the text.

A character is developed based on the given circumstances in the story and a way of being in the world justified in the script. We call it the five given circumstances, or the "5 Ws" — who, what, when, where and why. The specifics of how a person moves, speaks, evolves within the world of the story is in the text's given circumstances. The best actors are going to do a script analysis breakdown for every scene in which they appear. Consider their preproduction breakdown part of the rehearsal process. Because you will be shooting out of sequence, script preparation such as this becomes essential for the continuity of the character's story arc and the actor's performance.

As a director you must get used to answering questions about motivation: Why does each characters do what they do? It's become a bit of a joke on-set: "What's my motivation?" Yet, motivation is key. When an actor knows why a character does something, it makes emotional sense, and the actor can take the character where it needs to go. Your job as director is to give her something to do (an action, a verb) that physicalizes that motivation. (See Resources: Judith Weston's *Directing Actors*.)

Also in the actor's toolbox you'll find qualities, or "states of listening" — physical activities, relationship, actions and objectives, beats, text analysis, and so on. A good actor is going to explore the text and make choices that are informed by the text and justified by the text. A good actor is going to do research on a character so that when they show up on-set the first day of rehearsal, they have choices to show you. A good actor is going to do homework.

One of the main reasons you want to give scripts to actors prior to an audition is to evaluate just what kind of actor you have standing in front of you: one who is flying by the seat of his pants, or prepared with choices and some understanding of how this character functions within your story; the one who might leave your shot-list up to chance, or the one that has done his homework.

So let us agree that acting is subjective. What I like might not be what you like. Who I select for a role might not be who you would select. Fine.

However, you do need to understand the casting process so you can get better at it. Casting better actors makes better movies, no matter what your budget. You need to learn how to spot the good, the bad and the ugly, and to dig for who is great. So, you need to understand a bit about the acting process.

EXERCISE: *Who Do You Like?*

Start by making a list of the actors whose work you really like and why. Do they transport you? How are they believable? What about this actor draws you in? Why do you like them? Are you responding to something emotional? Sexual? As a director you need to know what you like and why. You need to be able to look at an actor, put them through a reading and come out of the audition process with a clear understanding of how they work, how they would work with you directing them, and why they are right for the role.

EXERCISE: *Character Types.*

Next, make a list of actors you like by various character types:

TYPE	ACTOR	WHY
leading man/woman		
romantic lead, man/woman		
character lead, man/woman		
character comedian		
hero		
villain		
confidante (friend, sidekick)		
wise fool		
wise woman		

political/spiritual leader/teacher
shaman/magician
village idiot (psychotic)
clever servant
dumb servant

In the next column, why do you like them in these types of roles? Where are the patterns? Do you see how some actors get to play various types, while others play the same type over and over? Look to see who uses the tools to manipulate voice and body, states of listening, character and relationship to completely transform from one film to the next, and who doesn't.

Basic to script structure is character type. Character type is different than character function. Any character can be your protagonist or your antagonist, your foil or your comic relief. Character types function within your story in recognizable ways, which inform your audience. Understand who is your antagonist, who is your protagonist, and which one is the villain. Sometimes the villain is a job, or a situation, as in *The Perfect Storm*, where the weather is the villain. Some would say the villain in this picture is the character flaw in George Clooney's character of the captain: his ego. However, the title confirms that the villain is the weather. The captain hasn't set out to kill anyone, or do severe damage as does *Othello*'s Iago, or the lunatic *Natural Born Killers* who go on a shooting spree.

Combinations make the best characters because they are multi-dimensional. Here are a few character type combinations employed to great results:

Dustin Hoffman in *Rain Man*: village idiot + wise fool.
Jack Nicholson in *One Flew Over the Cuckoo's Nest*: village idiot + hero.
Harrison Ford as Indiana Jones: clever servant + lover + hero.
Sean Connery as James Bond: really clever servant + action hero + lover.
Kathy Bates in *Misery*: villain + village idiot.

Nicole Kidman in *The Hours*: wise woman + village idiot.
Faye Dunaway in *Bonnie and Clyde*: leading woman.
Johnny Depp in *Chocolat*: leading man.

EXERCISE: *Character type attributes.*

List attributes of each character type. For example:
   Villain: hateful, disloyal, shifty, untrustworthy, vengeful.
   Wise Woman: elder teacher, intellectual, caring, listener,
   kind.

ACTING 101 FOR DIRECTORS:
How you feel is a result of what you do.

As we wrap up our discussion of what constitutes great acting,
it is essential for directors to learn the tools of acting and the
vocabulary of great acting. Doing so will make you a better
director because you will be able to give direction that makes
sense to your actors. You will speak their language. And their
language is all about actions and objectives: What is a character doing to get what they want in a scene? When you give
actors things to do, you will stop telling them how to feel.
Actors respond to doing things, because feeling comes from
doing. How you feel (emotional content/connection) is a result
of what you do (action).

   Avoid giving directions that include telling actors how
they're supposed to feel. Feeling is a result, a reaction. In
other words, don't tell them the result. You want the result to
happen. You want moments to happen. If an actor is playing
the action that works, then the emotional content of the scene
is going to work. Help your actors find the action that is going
to produce the result, the response you need, the *reaction*, in
the moment, caught on camera.

A good actor experiments through rehearsal to find the right action for the desired emotional outcome, which is evident in the script. It is their job to give you an action that produces the desired emotional result. Don't tell them how or what to feel. You wouldn't tell your DP how to run his equipment. Don't do it with actors.

The key to giving actors "things to do" is verbs. Verbs are the action words of language. Find the right verb (action), and you will get the desired emotional content the scene needs. The feeling part is the magic; it is the response to the given circumstances in the moment that your camera is tuned in to pick up.

Look at the appendix in the back of Judith Weston's book, *Directing Actors*. Once you understand how action verbs fit into the actor's toolbox, you will be well on your way toward becoming a director actors will want to work with. Directing is a fine art and requires skill, leadership, communication and finesse. Communicating with actors, understanding how they work, is essential to better casting decisions.

Work on it. In time you'll be better able to make suggestions and give direction during the audition to better evaluate what kind of actor you have in front of you. You will learn how to talk to actors in their language and how to determine if this is someone you can work with: an actor who can give you exactly what you see in your head. You do want it out of your head and up there on the stage or on the screen, don't you?

Understanding the craft: where to go for help.

If this discussion on actions and feeling isn't making much sense to you, perhaps one of the best things you can do for your directing career is to take an acting class, a good one. And by this I don't mean a marketing class taught by a casting director focusing on cold script reading or audition techniques. I mean an acting class where they work on scenes from plays and screenplays; a class where you break the

text into beats, work actions and objectives, explore relationship and characterization and states of listening. Great acting
teachers are in every city. Get online and check them out.
If you don't want to invest in a university-level course with
higher tuition, look into the community colleges in your area,
which are a great, affordable resource. The community college theatre departments in the United States have awesome
teachers. Anyone teaching at a community college has had
to jump through numerous hoops to get that job, and, more
than likely, have a Master's degree. Also, in every city there
are great studio classes where professional performers study.
Locate them through your local nonprofit theatre arts or film
service bureau. Be sure it's an acting/scene study class, not a
marketing/audition class.

If taking an acting class frightens you, most teachers do
allow audits. Avoid telling other students you're a director so
as not to affect class presentations and performances.

Spend half the time thinking about the acting process as
you do about your script, or which filters you're going to use
when, and you will make a better movie. Aren't there already
enough bad movies?

CHAPTER SIX

TIMELINES —
WHEN TO START AND
WHAT TO DO BEFORE
JUMPING IN

> "The funniest thing is that all the things every director goes through, I thought I could shortcut, but there was no getting around those issues." — GEORGE CLOONEY

Announcements, auditions, callbacks and contracts: AACC.

The casting process can be broken down into four parts: announcing the project with a casting breakdown, auditions, callbacks, and the offering of contracts. It might be two weeks or two months from announcing to offers. Commercials tend to take the shorter route along with television shows, which move through the entire process very quickly. When it comes to feature films, however, one of the biggest traps is failure to allow enough time for casting and callbacks prior to production. See what you can do to avoid traps and failures. Before you announce your auditions, you're going to need the following:

- A legitimate place to hold them.
- A staff to run them:
  - ✓ Someone running camera.
  - ✓ Someone on check-in/ushering actors in and out.
  - ✓ A reader. This person reads with the actor auditioning.
  - ✓ And you.

Your paperwork must be completed with the union office, and to complete the SAG paperwork you're going to need to know when you're shooting, your budget, and have your LLC and production insurance in place. Welcome to producing and pre-pro planning. See Chapter Five for more on SAG paperwork.

WHERE TO HOLD AUDITIONS

An appropriate place to hold auditions does not include the garage, your living room or a hotel room. They are not held in private homes or the backyard. These are red flags and actors will avoid coming to you and you'll end up casting whatever friends you have left. If you want to make a better movie, and who doesn't, you need to work with better actors. Better actors stay busy and can be choosy when it comes to working on low-budget shorts and features.

Auditions are held in studios, hotel conference rooms, rehearsal halls, etc. You need to find a public place with rest-rooms and parking or access to public transportation; the social hall of a church for example, or a hotel function room. One common place to hold an audition is the rehearsal room at a community theatre. Most cities have a theatre organization where you can find spaces to rent in the arts community for a reasonable fee. Colleges and universities often have very low rental rates to book a classroom. Vocational schools are another place to look. Office buildings have meeting rooms. Ask the people on your staff, your producer, if they work in an office building with a function room you could sign up.

Try your local library for conference rooms. Ask your friends where they held their auditions. Be sure it is clean and comfortable and has access to water and restrooms.

THE TIMELINE EXPLAINED

For large projects, such as feature films, we create a schedule by working backward from the approximate first day on-set. Begin with the first day of shooting and start making your lists of what you need to get done by when. For smaller projects, try switching "months" to "weeks" and "weeks" to "days."

Two weeks from first shoot date: Rehearsals.

After your first full-company "table read" (the entire cast reading the script out loud), you're going to want a week or two of rehearsals with your leading actors before you start shooting to figure out camera moves, where the close-ups are going to come, how you're going to cut each scene. Get used to it: Actors need rehearsal; actors love rehearsal; actors want rehearsals. No matter what anyone told you in film school, it's a really bad idea to have actors show up on the first day of shooting and their only rehearsal is a camera warm-up prior to the shot.

One month from first shoot date: Contracts.

Prior to rehearsals, you'll need to get the contracts signed. To get the contract signed you need approximate shooting days, which means you need your production breakdown completed and your locations secured. Be sure to review the SAG contract for specifics regarding putting hard shoot dates or approximate dates on a contract. Changing shoot dates after a confirmation can create all sorts of problems including fines, additional payroll, and scheduling nightmares for locations as well as competition with other productions for that actor. Also, to offer contracts SAG is going to need your budget, your script, a copy of your LLC, and a copy of your insurance policy. All of it takes time.

Six weeks from first shoot date: Callbacks.

Before you offer contracts, you'll have your final round of callbacks. After you've shifted through all the audition tapes and weeded out all the wannabes and checked references, you'll be calling back only the top three or four picks for each role. You may not get your first pick for all sorts of reasons: money, scheduling conflicts, personal emergencies. Always have a second or third choice you can live with, one who will work almost as well as your first choice.

Two months from first shoot date: Auditions.

Before callbacks, you'll have preliminary auditions and readings from the script. You'll need time to review submission materials. And in this day and age, technology is your best friend. Insist that actors send you links to sample footage online. It will save you a lot of time. See what someone looks like on camera before you bring them in for an audition. For principal casting, open calls are not necessary. Prescreen actors with headshots, resumes and online reels, all sent to your inbox. Set up your first round of auditions with only those actors who are qualified, ready and right for the roles you are casting. The only time you'll ever really need or want to hold an open call is if you need a lot of background extras. Avoid them. Any actor on the ball is out there every day looking for new audition announcements. Your announcement will be distributed to all the online sites and the actors will find you. You also have been developing relationships with talent agents who will send you submissions. Let us save that for another chapter.

Ten weeks from first shoot date:
Distributing audition information.

Even with all the bulletin boards out there online, it is a good idea to allow a couple of weeks for your information to spread around. Word-of-mouth also will help attract the best actors.

The day your announcement goes active, be ready for submissions to come pouring in. Be ready with email accounts that can handle attachments and footage files. Be ready to download and get your files organized. (See Chapter Six for document workflow suggestions.) After your cut-off date, give yourself another three or four days to respond via email to those actors you want to meet, schedule and confirm.

Three months from first shoot date: Preproduction breakdown.

You can't put the audition information out to the world if you don't have some idea of when and where you're shooting. Actors reading your breakdown will immediately determine if this sounds like something they want to be involved in. By a certain age and level of experience, actors don't really need another low-budget independent movie on their resume for "copy, credit, meals." What they do need is a great role that could propel their careers by getting into the right film festival. So smart actors today are going to look at your background, your track record, what festivals you've been in, and who you've worked with.

To get from announcing your casting breakdown to your first day on-set, there is a lot to do. What you really need is a good producer. If you bring a producer onboard, be sure to ask in the interview if they have any experience with SAG contracts. It is essential that you get your paperwork completed correctly and on time.

TIMELINE RECAP

To summarize, your timeline looks like this:
- Three months from first shoot date: Preproduction breakdown.
- Ten weeks from first shoot date: Audition information distribution.

■ Two months from first shoot date: Auditions.

■ Six weeks from first shoot date: Callbacks.

■ One month from first shoot date: Contracts.

■ Two weeks from first shoot date: Rehearsals.

UNION PREPARATION RECAP

■ Your SAG checklist:

■ Production budget

■ Final script

■ Proof of production insurance

■ LLC documents

■ Production dates

■ Names and membership numbers of SAG actors

✓ Avoid mistakes by not rushing. Always have a Plan B: you may not get your first-pick actor.

✓ Audition days run late and get backed up when you fail to allow enough time per person.

CHAPTER SEVEN

THE CASTING BREAKDOWN —
SPREADING THE WORD

"It is the attention to details that separates the good, the bad and the ugly from the courageous, brilliant and exceptional." — HESTER SCHELL, *writer/director*

"Our feeling is that the most important thing on a set is that actors have enough confidence to try different things. If there's stress or tension, they won't go out on a limb because they won't want to embarrass themselves if they don't feel completely comfortable." — PETER FARRELLY

Directors Speak: In Session

" I learned that as the creative leader, it's a good idea to have staff repeat back to me what I just asked them to do and clarify instructions. Too often subordinates interpret what you said you needed or misquote you to a vendor. We got bleu cheese on the pizza instead of blue chintz on the sofa. Communication and leadership is more than half the battle. Great casting is surely more than the other half. "

■ ■ ■ ■ ■

" They allowed me to see who they were, who I'd be working with. They didn't walk in with bravado or a false compensating level of confidence, nor did they look like they were about to die. Happy, but not too happy. The best thing an actor can do at an audition is to be a well-balanced, normal person who I want to work with, someone who cares about how they look (they didn't roll out of bed and are now standing in front of me) and cares what I think about what they are presenting me. "

BREAKDOWN ELEMENTS

The casting announcement, commonly referred to as the "breakdown," is just that: a breakdown of the essential information actors would need to know to determine their suitability for your project and whether the schedule would work for them. It's an invitation to join a team. Craft your breakdown in such a way as to inspire confidence by showing you know what you're doing. Create interest and intrigue so people will want to work with you. Make it exciting.

How you present your breakdown to the world reflects on how you will run your set. Actors are going to be looking you up on *imdb.com* and other film social networking websites. No one has time to get involved with an unorganized film. It is the attention to details that separates the good, the bad and the ugly from the courageous, brilliant and exceptional. Always proofread your announcements. Misspellings, poor punctuation and grammatical errors are red flags suggesting that you're not on top of things.

Casting announcements typically contain the following information:

TITLE — "Untitled" is fine if you don't know yet. You can also follow the title with (Working Title).

PRODUCER — Who is responsible for this project.

DIRECTOR — You. Include one or two notable festivals/awards, other critical successes, or a website where applicants can see your reel. They're going to check you out too.

DESCRIPTION — Include the genre of the movie and your log line, with a brief story synopsis. Keep it short. Include your anticipated rating and any union affiliation. If nudity is required for a particular role, you need to state clearly the amount and style of nudity. Mention the shot list if you can.

FORMAT — This refers to film stock, digital, or media. It's nice to know if you're shooting HD, SD, RED or whatever the next "it" format is. Another clue actors look for is whether you are shooting on film. Film budgets are bigger, and the expected quality is higher. There is a different excitement on-set when working with the real thing.

ROLES — Include: name, age range, ethnicity and character adjectives, special requirements such as nudity, etc. Indicate size of roles: Leads, Supporting, Extras. CAPITALIZE CHARACTER NAMES. Include approximately how many days on-set each character requires. Actors will sometimes only apply for supporting roles because they know that they can't fit a lead into their schedules. Include as much information as you can. Here are role sizes from smallest to largest: Extra/Background, Featured Extra/Featured Bit, Stand-In, Under-Five, Day Player, Guest Star (TV), Supporting, Co-Star (TV), Lead, Star. Age Ranges break down into natural stages of life: Infant, Toddler, Child (4-10), Adolescent (11-13), Teen (13-18), Adult (25-40), Mature Adult (45-65), and Senior (70+).

Include any details that will help clarify what you need. If you're leading actor is six feet tall, and you need a romantic partner, or you have two leads in a lot of two shots, pay attention to height.

CREW - If you're still looking, you may as well include it here. It can't hurt.

SUBMISSION PROCEDURES — This means how actors reach you and where to send headshots, resumes and reels — or, if you're having people call to schedule an interview, when and who to call for an appointment. Or if it's NO CALLS PLEASE. Include the dates of the auditions, whether you are holding an open call with the location and time of the call, as well as what you require such as a short one-minute monologue. Also, it's important to include a submissions deadline. A time span of about two weeks is common and generous. Shorter or longer is acceptable. Be sure to remove your announcement at deadline, unless you want late submissions. (Experience says to keep the window open. I had a great actor submit for a role after the deadline. He got a callback.)

PAY/PERKS — If you make an effort to pay something in addition to covering expenses, such as gas, bridge tolls, parking, food, etc., you will attract more qualified actors with experience. Let them know what kind of contract you are working under: SAG Modified Low-budget, Experimental, Student, SAG Ultra Low-budget, etc.

SHOOT DATES — Be as specific as you can about shoot dates. If you don't know yet, approximate. For example: weekends July through September.

ADDITIONAL DETAILS — Actors need to know your general shooting location, so include what you know about your locations. If you are working in languages other than English, let people know. Details also include anything from "you need a passport, we are shooting two days in Mexico/Canada" to "extreme horror and makeup special effects will require two hours a day in the makeup chair," or anything other information you feel actors might want to know up front. If there are any major award-winners on the team, mention them here as well as any major film festivals where you have had a screening. For example, if you've had three features in CineQuest or Berlin, actors will know a bit about your track record.

You started casting in your head as you read the final draft of the script. You've formed an idea of what each person looks like.

HOMEWORK

Make a list of known actors you see in the role. Now find someone similar to that actor in age, color, style and delivery.

Get rid of any assumptions you have about who you can or can't afford. There are so many types of contacts now, from deferred pay to SAG Ultra Low-budget that you really can afford to work with professionals. Can't remember who the actor was in that movie you like so much? Go to *imdb.com* and search away. The Internet Movie Database. Use it. It's your friend.

SAMPLE BREAKDOWNS

The first sample breakdown below refers actors to another website for the character details, which is a great idea. Please note the clean and concise character descriptions in these samples.

Sample Breakdown 1

TITLE: DISCLOSURE

PRODUCERS: XXXXXXX and XXXXXX XXXXXXXXX

DIRECTOR: XXXXXXXX

DESCRIPTION: Feature, shooting in Northern California. Contemporary Sci-fi thriller.

LOGLINE: Respected Silicon Valley blogger puts his reputation and life on the line after he uncovers an alien presence that threatens to undermine our high tech-dependent society.

FORMAT: HD 1080P — shooting with Canon 5D Mark II

PROCEDURE: Review supporting roles online here: URL.com Auditions: xxx, 2010, 10am to 3pm, in (name your city here,) plus one evening session TBA. Please follow these specific submission details for Headshot/resume/reel submissions:

— If you are a match, please submit headshots/resumes and URL to ONLINE Footage to: xxxx@youremail.com. Director must see how you look on film prior to booking an audition. There will NOT be an open call.

— Please put the title and the character in the subject line of your email. DISCLOSURE: (Character you wish to read for)

— If you don't have a demo reel online, send a clip no longer than 1 minute. We cannot prescreen you without a clip. Do not email entire shorts or entire scenes.

— Be sure your email address book is set to INCLUDE our address: xxxx@youremail.com as we try very hard to get back to everyone who submits. If you don't hear back from us, be sure to check your trash and spam files and set your filters. We look forward to receiving your materials. Please no phone calls.

ROLES:

LEAD — Already cast. "Name known actor" will play the lead.

SUPPORTING ROLES: Character Details here:

yourmoviewebsite.com/detailedcharacterdescriptionshere.html

Submission deadline: September 24, 2011.

SHOOT DATES: Late November including Thanksgiving Weekend, but NOT on Thanksgiving Day, through Mid-December, wrapping before the holidays.

PAY/PERKS: SAG Ultra Low-budget agreement ($100/day plus SAG benefits). Non-union, $100/day. Copy, credit, meals, gas for all actors.

This breakdown went into great detail about reel submissions, and it was very specific about expectations. Next, these two breakdowns do a great job with character descriptions:

SAMPLE BREAKDOWN 2

PROJECT: BIG, BAD MOON

PRODUCER: XXX XXXX

DESCRIPTION: Two weeks ago, a giant asteroid slammed into the moon, driving it closer to Earth. Ray, a remorseful ex-con, and his two down-and-out brothers are forced to take in Harry — their once abusive but now catatonic father — who has been discharged from the hospital. Tonight, as the first full moon rises since the asteroid impact, strange and terrifying things begin to happen. Not the least of which — Harry wakes up.

FORMAT: HD, Feature length.

ROLES:

RAY TEMPLETON: Caucasian, 40-45, divorced, one-time ex-con, self-deprecating, resilient, car salesman. The eldest and most responsible of three adult sons.

HARRY TEMPLETON: Caucasian, 65-70, hard-as-nails former Marine combat vet. Great Marine, terrible father, dry sense of humor.

TOBY TEMPLETON: Caucasian, 35-40, serio-comic relief, borderline psychotic, appears not too bright but can be clever in his insults, eager to go... anywhere.

MARNIE MAYS: 30-35, mousy-at-first victim of abusive husband but becomes a fighter. Very kind-hearted mother of a little girl.

KIRK FREEMAN: early-20s, steely-eyed and confident ROTC squad leader. "Lunar Effect": Paranoia turns him into uber-leader/soldier.

LON TEMPLETON: late-20s to early-30s, gay, hippie-like, bearded, long haired vegan youngest of the brothers. "Lunar Effect": He thinks he's a werewolf.

ABDUL ALLOWANI: Middle-eastern, 50s, humorless old-world thinker.

MAJALE ALLOWANI: Middle-eastern, 40s, beautiful but oppressed wife of Abdul. "Lunar Effect": Comes out from under her burka.

WALTER KNAPP: 30s, the nerdish, bullied neighbor. "Lunar Effect": comes way out of his shell and finds his inner Tony Robbins-meets-Michael Meyers.

SAMIR ALLOWANI: Middle-eastern, early-20s, Abdul's volatile son and band leader of the "Jihad Genies".

MADDY MAYS: Caucasian, 10-12, Marnie's tomboy daughter who enjoys violent video games a bit too much.

TUCKER MAYS: Caucasian, 30s, Marnie's abusive husband. "Lunar Effect": Takes abuse to a higher level.

FACILITATOR: female, 50s, frumpy, New Ager leader of Anger Management Group.

Other roles:

ROTC cadets, early 20s, all nationalities.

TWO NEWLYWEDS: early 20s.

ELDERLY WOMAN: 70s

INDIAN STORE CLERK, 30s-50s,

SUBMISSION PROCEDURE: Please submit headshots online to: XXXXXXX xxx@email.com as well as XXX XXXXXXXX xxxxx@youremail.com.

Or by mail to Your Company Name Productions, 1234 Street or POB address, Your City, State, Zip.

OTHER INFO: Please visit our website for information regarding our company. This is our fourth no-budget Indie feature. We're fun & easygoing but professional & get things done right. your-website.com

We're also looking for a few non-paid crew positions: Prop/Set Designer, Producer assistants, camera assistant, boom operator. Immediate help needed for preproduction. Serious inquiries only please. No experience required.

PAY/PERKS: Copy, credits, festival exposure.

Notice how specific these descriptions are, and they're short. They include the age range and ethnicity, as well as how the character functions within the story. This tells me they know about story structure.

SAMPLE BREAKDOWN 3

PROJECT: 1.5

PRODUCER: XXXXXX XXXXXX

DESCRIPTION: Genre: Coming of Age / Diaspora / Drama

TRT: 12 minutes

Logline: Unsure of his role in life within the U.S., Korean immigrant teenager Il-Oh travels inward and outward to escape the grip of his father and find an answer to his identity.

Synopsis: Il-Oh (19), a Korean-American teenager back from his first year of college, is working part-time at his father's grocery store over the summer. Born and raised in Korea but having spent the last 7 years in the U.S., Il-Oh had realized that he can't exactly fit into either group; he is yet to feel entirely comfortable around Americans, and fails to keep up with the Koreans and their rapidly changing pop culture. His frustration, aimed mainly and misguidedly at his father, builds up and eventually leads to an enraged outburst. In the end, Il-Oh finally learns that his particular situation and surroundings are not barriers, but rather gifts of the present that propel him towards a brighter future.

Rated PG/PG-13. Non-union, no nudity.

FORMAT: HD Video

ROLES:

Lead Role:

IL-OH KIM (19) is a Korean immigrant who had come to the U.S.with his father SUK-HOON when he was 12 years old. After his freshman year in college, where he had had trouble finding a comfortable group he could fit into, Il-Oh opts to work at his father's grocery store over the summer. Feeling estranged from both his Korean and American friends, Il-Oh lets out his frustration upon Suk-Hoon, who takes this as disrespectful.

Co-Star:

SUK-HOON KIM (48) came to the U.S. with his son and has been running WOORI FOODS, a Korean grocery store for 4 years. Since the death of his wife, Suk-Hoon has tried to take on the nurturing maternal role, but is not used to showing affection towards his son; the inexperience often translates into awkwardness. A strong patriot, Suk-Hoon has pride in his native country of Korea and wishes to pass that heritage on to his son, but at the same time wants Il-Oh to find his own way living in the U.S.

Supporting Roles:

ANDY PARK (20) is Il-Oh's high school friend. Though of Korean heritage, being born and raised in the U.S. makes Andy anything but Korean. He does not speak Korean but can understand it rather well. He fashions baggy hip-hop clothes and lives a decadent life of debauchery.

ERICA VENTON (19) is an attractive, outgoing, gregarious cheerleader-type girl with strong sex appeal. She is aggressive in getting what she wants.

PROCEDURE: Please submit headshot and resume to xxxxxx@ googlegroups.com

PAY/PERKS: Lunches will be provided on-set. Stipends to be decided.

SHOOT DATES: Sep. 11-13, 2009.

Here they mention "stipends to be decided." This is nice to know that they are paying actors something. It is important to understand why your budget must compensate and cover expenses. It builds respect. Avoid paying crew members something and actors nothing. Think about what this says about your priorities. Also notice they've said "Non-union, no nudity." It is only necessary to mention nudity when there is nudity, so leave out "no nudity." When there is nudity, include the shot list. For example, in the first sample breakdown above, actors are referred to another website for all the specifics about the character descriptions. Here you would find that nudity is required for one role, along with very specific shot list: bath tub scene, full frontal waist up; full back shot; wrapped in towel shot. Also included would be this: sensitive and sensual to story, hetero. This is a simple way to let people know the nature of the nudity if there is any romance and if it is gay, straight, lesbian or transgender.

BREAKDOWN DISTRIBUTION

Do you want to keep it local, or do a national outreach? If you're casting a festival short with just a few roles, keep it local. If you are casting a feature you will want to see everyone available with experience including A- and B-list names, those working in television, or coming up through the comedy clubs. You will want to prescreen as many actors as possible and will have to weed through the inexperienced and the untrained to find them, or pay a casting director to do that for you. It's time-consuming and gets tedious, but you must have courage and cast your net upon the open sea.

National.

The Internet has leveled the playing field and it is no longer impossible to get the attention of the agents in New York City and Los Angeles. If you post to the nationally recognized casting websites, they will see it, or the assistant will see it, but more importantly, the actor will see it. Actors know where to look for legitimate work. Add this to your submission procedure guidelines: "agency submissions accepted."

At each of these websites you will be required to register and create a profile. They are in business to list auditions, so it is in their interest to work with you and post your project.

The national reaching breakdown posting services include:
actorsaccess.com
breakdownservices.com
castingnetworks.com
mandy.com
nowcasting.com

There are others, but these are the top nationally known services regularly used. Several of these sites have local areas as well. By using all of these listing services you will have a goldmine of headshot/resume/reel submissions. You will go through all the submissions and select who you most want to call in for an audition. In your breakdown you indicated what you want to see in the audition: a reading from the script or a short monologue.

Local and Regional.

If you have decided not to go national with your breakdown distribution, you will need to resource websites that are regional. For example, in the San Francisco Bay Area, there is Bay Area Casting News (*bayareacasting.com*) that has built its reputation by servicing only Bay Area film projects. In the Boston area, there is *newenglandfilm.com*. In Portland, there are the Oregon Media Production Association and *oregonmedianet-work.org*. Every city has its own particular local media sites. Check with your state's film commission for local resources.

Notice I haven't mentioned Craigslist. While this site may be great for selling a car or finding an apartment — I've used it many times and love Craigslist — this may not be your best choice for posting film casting calls when there are so many other film- and media-specific routes to follow. Many actors have learned not to check Craigslist due to the resulting spam and questionable content of some listings. You need to post where the actors regularly look. There are a lot of postings for crew in the "Gigs" area.

Search and join the burgeoning online industry-related groups, such as Yahoo! and *indieclub.com*, both nationally reaching resources. Also, crew search *mandy.com* and *media-match.com*, among others for job postings. Chances are you've already collected people you like to work with for your crew. Most of us hire crew from people we know and have worked with previously.

Social Networking.

Utilize all the social networking sites (Facebook, MySpace, LinkedIn) to get your casting breakdown out to your email lists and groups. Look into the jobs posting section on *linkedin. com*. You will find dozens of film-related groups to join and build your community.

FLYERS: OTHER PLACES TO PUT YOUR BREAKDOWN

Because not everything happens on the Internet, make a flyer and post it on local college campuses in the film and theatre departments if you are willing to work with students. Campuses have a plethora of bulletin boards. It is likely you will need to put a date stamp on the flyer. Bookstore and café bulletin boards are also a great place for people to see your flyer. Attend film industry-related conferences. Mention your project to everyone in your address book.

Since every film needs a website to build audience and generate "buzz," one of the best places is right there on your movie's website. This will greatly reduce the information you put on your flyer. Simply state: "Casting Info Here..." with your URL.

Press releases.

Start working your marketing machine with your local community newspaper: Announce casting to your local community newspaper. Learn the appropriate format and write a good press release. Find out who edits the calendar page and get your open call listed. Many newspapers have a features editor who might show interest in doing a story on you and your project. Send the press release to your local news stations as well.

CONTACTING AGENTS

Let us begin by clearly defining the difference between agents and casting directors: Casting directors work for a production, and are paid on a contract basis by a producer. Agents represent actors and are paid commission, usually 10% of the total, by the actor.

If you are talking to agents, then you have a budget. If you decide to submit to agents because you want one of their clients in your movie, thoroughly research the submission guidelines for the agency and follow the instructions. If you don't have a budget to pay actors, avoid calling agents. If you aren't paying actors, there isn't anything to take 10% out of and therefore they have little to no interest in submitting their clients to you and your movie.

If your budget affords only a SAG Ultra Low-budget of $100 a day, it is unlikely that agents are going to work with you for $10 for each day an actor is on-set. More likely, you will be working with agents when you have a contract that makes it worth their time to do business with you. When you are paying "Scale + 10" (plus 10%), or a known actor's minimum on regular and fully budgeted projects, then you will need to know how to approach agents. When you get to this point and haven't hired a casting director, or you've got a real and healthy budget, be sure you are ready to swim with the sharks; your casting net just got really big. You only get one shot at getting it right. Agents are used to working with casting directors. This is changing as more directors do their own casting. Again, it is up to whether you are paying actors enough to warrant an agent doing business with you.

Even if you don't have a budget you may still be able to get this actor onboard. If the actor has seen your breakdown, contact them directly from their submission. Ultimately it is up to the actor to say "Yes" to you. In other words, many actors with fantastic television, film and festival credits (and, in some cases, even awards) will "self-submit" to projects, going around their agents, as is their right to do. If schedules permit and you can get this actor booked when he isn't doing other paid work, then you've just worked the system to your advantage. If this actor has not self-submitted to you and the agent has declined to respond due to money issues, find a way to get your breakdown and your script into the hands of the actor you want. Never give up. Be inventive. It happens every day.

Who represents whom.

There are a few ways to find out who represents and/or manages a particular actor. If your budget allows, join IMDb Pro and you can look up representation online there.

At the national SAG office in Los Angeles, there is a number to call to find out who represents your actor. Visit *sag.org* for the current number if you have trouble with this one: (800) 503-6737. (While you are there, click on services and review what else SAG can help you with.) Do your homework and be ready with your list of names in front of you when you pick up the phone. SAG will tell you who represents that actor. Ask for the number. Or, now that you know the agent, you can use other resources to look up actors' agency contacts, such as The Hollywood Creative Directory and The Ross Reports.

When you call the agent's office or group, ask for that agent's assistant. State that you are casting a feature (or commercial, short, whatever it is) and wish to know the script submission procedures for that actor. Depending on how busy that actor is will determine how far you get. Follow their instructions, and do your follow-up. How badly do you want that actor in your movie? Find out how far ahead that actor is scheduled. Find out if they do low-budget Indie films. Reach out but don't pester. Professional follow-up is an art.

Or, hire a casting director who knows the waters and how to cast the net. If you can't afford that, follow the established procedures when talking to agents. If you're ready to be talking to agents, you are ready to have a casting director do it for you. Agents return phone calls to casting directors. Agents develop relationships with casting directors. To agents, you're another unknown director who wants someone cheap. Your job is to make it worth their time to talk with you.

To get a perspective on this, do the math. If Nicole Kidman gets 12 million for a picture, how much is her agent getting? If Julia Roberts gets 20 million for a picture, how much is that agent getting? That's more than a year's salary for most of us — and then some — on one client for one project. Money doesn't talk — it screams!

When your budget can afford it, hire a casting director to connect with names and negotiate in your favor. They know how to work the ropes. They know who to call and how to handle the call. But if you choose to swim with the sharks, you need to know what the water temperature is and where the shark cage is located.

CHAPTER EIGHT

STAYING ORGANIZED

> "Eighty percent of success is showing up."
> — WOODY ALLEN

WORKFLOW

You've composed your breakdown, and posted to either regional/local or national online posting services, and the submissions are starting to come in. You created a deadline, so you can go into your account at each website and take the announcement down if you get overwhelmed. With a budget, you may even have a few agents to talk to, and things are moving along.

In the breakdown under "submission procedure" you were clear with what you wanted sent in. The standard is a head-shot/resume and includes a demo reel QuickTime file or a link to where you can view their footage. The simplest and most efficient way is to request a click-through hypertext link along with the email submission so you don't have to sift through downloads and save files.

Who follows instructions.

It's going to amaze you how people don't read details. So pay attention: Notice if someone has forgotten to include a link.

If an actor can't follow simple submission instructions, will she be able to get to the set on time? If their headshot isn't professional to industry standards (color, face and shoulders, in focus, name and contact information on the front) do they know enough about the film industry to be on your set? See Chapter Four for more on industry standards.

On a feature film I cast, I received submissions from out of the area for a SAG Ultra Low-budget, paying $100 a day, on a Local Hires Only. Translate: we were not covering airfare or hotel. When you do the math, it makes no sense for an actor to travel from out of town when the breakdown clearly states "Local Hires Only." You will still get those submissions. Just try to be kind.

Turn on your "Flake Radar."

It is your job to weed out the flakes, the prima donnas, egomaniacs, nutcases and wannabes who make mistakes and cause problems. Pay attention to your radar. If you suspect someone is a nutcase, move on. If someone can't follow directions by sending in the requested materials, get to the audition on time, etc., and you still hire them, you have yourself to blame when the same behavior shows up late on-set against the setting sun while you're about to miss your shot. Going through the casting procedures will give you ample time to evaluate work habits, reliability and consistency.

During casting, another director friend asks himself whether this is "someone I would want to go camping with. Are they fun, amiable and cooperative? After ten hours on-set, is this someone who has a sense of humor that is going to hold up? If the answer is 'No' it is unlikely I will give them a callback." Excellent advice, isn't it?

MANAGING FILES

On the first few days of your active posting, as submissions begin to come in, expect a lot of email. Do the necessary email homework: be sure attachments are allowed for medium to large files. If someone does send you a QuickTime file instead of a link, you'll need your computer to be equipped to accept the attachment. You'll want a generic email account. Manage your addresses as you go so that you may easily create the assorted email lists you'll need when responding to large numbers of people — assorted rejects, assorted callbacks, etc. Setting up a group is an excellent way of managing your email addresses. The point is, you must create this address book as you go, sorting into "Yes" and "No" piles.

From your "Yes" email, take your time getting through all the responses. Take a break after every 10 to 15 submissions to stay refreshed and keep your perspective alive and awake. For each actor you want to see, click on SAVE or SAVE ATTACHMENTS. Create a folder using their *name and the role name.* Save the attachments into that folder. Put all the actor folders into a larger folder called *Headshots, Resumes and Reels/ Links.* Put this folder into another folder called *CASTING: (Project Title).* Start out organized to stay organized. It will look like this:

CASTING: (PROJECT TITLE)
    Headshot/Resumes/Reels and Links
        Actor Joe
            Resume
            Photo
            Link to online footage
        Actor Jane
            Resume
            Photo
            Link to online footage

You now have a casting folder, and inside that your project folder, and inside that folder a folder for each person you are considering with the actor's name and the role they are up for. As you eliminate candidates, you can delete folders, or better yet, move them to your backup drive to save headshots. There will be another project one day and the actor who is not right for this project may be right the next time.

Confirming auditions.

Email makes it easy to confirm auditions. Compose a generic response and fill in the actor's name and potential role. Or do bulk email and refer people to the website for all the details you've uploaded online. This saves a huge amount of time. As a reminder, and to thwart email spam, remember to use your Blind Carbon Copy (BCC:) setting on your email.

Dear_____

Thank you for submitting your materials for (PROJECT TITLE). We would like to read you for the role of (CHARACTER). Attached, please find the sides to prepare. At your earliest convenience, please send your best two available time slots on (DAY, DATE), between the hours of (WHEN TO WHEN). We will make every attempt to get you one of these preferred time slots based on your preferences.

Please bring a headshot and resume to the audition. The auditions will be at (COMPLETE PHYSICAL ADDRESS WITH ZIP CODE). The closest (BUS/TRAIN/SUBWAY) is _____. By car, parking is on the street, or the nearest paid lot is (LOCATION).

We look forward to meeting you. If you have any questions, please email us. Please no phone calls. We will contact you with a confirmation on your preferred time slot.

Regards,

Casting — (PROJECT TITLE)

Production Company

Maintaining friendly professional email is easy. Including complete instructions, a map, parking information and details will ensure that your prospects arrive prepared and on time. As actors respond to email with additional questions, you can hit your reply button and then your signature button which includes "For more information, parking, directions and location of the audition, please click here: (YOUR WEBSITE)."

HANDLING REJECTIONS

Actors are accustomed to rejection. It's a common occurrence that either drives them from the business or builds very thick skin. Most of the time we are dealing with sane people who understand that 90% of the time they're not going to get the role. Actors send off submissions and when they don't hear anything, assume they are not getting an audition. So it's nice for those actors you don't wish to meet to know their status. Compose a simple, polite email and send it to everyone you are not going to invite to see you. Here is a sample:

"Thank you for your submission to our project. If we need any additional information we will be in touch."

Or,

"We have received your submission for (PROJECT TITLE), and while we appreciate hearing from you, we are not able to offer you an audition at this time. Good luck with all your endeavors."

Actors just want to know what happens to all the submissions they send. Email programs have signature functions and auto responders, so learn to use them. Remember to be kind. People just want to know what's going on.

OTHER FILES

Now that you have your master casting folder inside your main project folder, let us look and see what else you want in there.

Creating script sides from your screenplay.

At some point you will choose what scenes to read in your casting sessions, and you will need to email these "sides" to each actor. SAG requires a 24-hour notice. A few days are wonderful and a week is awesome.

Open up your screenplay and make those scene selections. When deciding which scenes to read, stick to the pivotal moments. Find the pages of dialogue that create connections between characters. If you have a lot of monologues in your script, choose one for each character.

Open a new file in your screenwriting software and title it SIDES: Character Name, Scene 1. Copy the scene from the screenplay and paste it into your side file. All your formatting will copy. If you copy from your screenwriting software into another program, you will loose your formatting. Stick to your writing program. Place all the scenes in one folder titled: SIDES. If you have another scene for the same character, call it SIDES: Character Name, Scene 2. Create a side focusing on each leading and supporting character in your breakdown that has lines.

Next, through your computer's print menu, create a PDF version of each side. This is essential because they're not going to have your script software, so they won't be able to open the file unless you save it as a PDF.

Sign-in sheets.

Make a simple sign-in sheet. With readings from the script at your first round of auditions, you are looking at seeing one actor about every 10 minutes. Below is a basic template to get you started. Have your gatekeeper check them in and make notes. You can also use it to make a check mark if you want to call someone back.

Welcome!
PLEASE SIGN-IN

DATE of AUDITION
PRODUCTION COMPANY: PROJECT

please print legibly:

NAME	TIME IN TIME OUT	UNION STATUS/ AGENT	EMAIL	MOBILE/ BEST TIME TO CALL
----	----	----	----	----
----	----	----	----	----
----	----	----	----	----
----	----	----	----	----
----	----	----	----	----
----	----	----	----	----
----	----	----	----	----

Figure 2: Sample Sign-In Sheet

The schedule is different than the sign-in sheet. This is what your schedule will look like:

TIME	ACTOR/ROLE	IN/OUT	NOTES (Callback — Y/N)
10:00			
10:10			
10:20			
10:30			

You will need to contact the SAG office for the SAG sign-in sheet for members only. Fill out the top portion only. As SAG actors arrive they will sign-in and note their actual appointment time. On their way out, they sign out. You will return this file to the SAG office along with other required paperwork. See Figure 2.

SCREEN ACTORS GUILD THEATRICAL & TELEVISION SIGN-IN SHEET #20

PRODUCER:_____ CASTING REP:_____
PROD'N CO:_____ CASTING REP. PHONE:_____
PROD'N OFFICE PRODUCTION TITLE:_____
PHONE #_____ EPISODE:_____

AUDITION DATE:_____

Casting Director's Signature

CASTING REP:
Please fill in [time seen]
for each actor

(1) NAME	(2) SAG MEMBER NUMBER	(3) ROLE	(4) AGENT	(5) PROVIDED?		(6) ARRIVAL TIME	(7) APPT. TIME	(8) TIME SEEN (Req. req.)	(9) TIME OUT	(10) TAPED?	(11) ACT. INI.
				PARK	SCRIPT						

REVISED 3/96

Figure 3: SAG Sign-In Sheet

MASTER SPREADSHEET

Saving the most important file for last, be ready to start a spreadsheet as your submissions come in. Avoid letting the email pile up to transfer information later. You risk missing someone. Add to the spreadsheet as you select actors you want to audition. Do not put anyone on the spreadsheet you are not meeting.

I recommend Excel. As files are emailed only to staff who need the information, eliminate risk of unwanted changes by saving as a PDF file and sending only this. Save the master file for your use only. Also, check movie production software. You may prefer to skip Excel and work directly in Movie Magic. Excel also creates hypertext so you can jump over to an actor's website and review footage directly from the spreadsheet. You will also make notes about union status and where their home base is so you can carefully pay attention to who is eligible to work as a local hire and who isn't. Unions are very specific with contracts and insist on perfect records.

ROLE	ACTOR	PHONE	WEB LINK/ FOOTAGE	EMAIL
		NU = Non Union SAG = Screen Actors Guild		
MEN				

Start at the top of a new page for each character. Include any other details that will help you easily access how to reach people. Have one section for men, women or children. Only put the actors you plan on meeting onto the spreadsheet. The others go in the reject pile. Do your best to stay organized from the start.

Because we often have union actors in the leading and major supporting roles and non-union actors in smaller supporting roles and bit parts, include union status on the spreadsheet. You will need to easily access who is a local actor and who is coming from out of town and needs a *per diem*, airfare and hotel.

This spreadsheet will eventually evolve into your cast contact sheet. As you select individuals for a callback, you can highlight that row. As you eliminate actors after first-rounds auditions and callbacks, you can select their line and hit delete. Anyone not called back can be deleted. By the time you finish casting, you'll only have those left who you wish to offer a role.

Here is an index of typical files to keep you organized:

Main Folder — CASTING: Project Title
    Folder: Headshot/Resumes/Reels and Links
        Folder: Each actor
            File: Resume
            File: Photo
            File: Link to online footage
    Folder: SIDES
        File: SIDES: Character Name, Scene 1.
        File: SIDES: Character Name, Scene 2.
        File: SIDES: Character Name, Scene 3.
    File: Full Script PDF
    Folder: Contacts
        File: Crew
        File: Actors
        File: Vendors
        File: Excel Spreadsheet

THE FIRST ROUND –
WHAT YOU NEED AND
WHERE YOU NEED IT

"Acting is not about being someone different. It's finding the similarity in what is apparently different, then finding myself in there. I'm curious about other people. That's the essence of my acting. I'm interested in what it would be like to be you." — MERYL STREEP

"A writer's contribution is literary and a film is not literary. When you take that stuff off the page and cast the people who are going to fit into those roles, that's what being a director is." — TAYLOR HACKFORD

Actors Speak: In Session

❝ The worst that ever happened to me? Smoking in the audition room. Just before I went in to sing they had been smoking. The small room was filled with smoke. So inconsiderate. I would never want to work with them. ❞

■ ■ ■ ■ ■

❝ The worst thing in any audition process is to show overt preference for someone who is auditioning. This irritates everyone who notices it. Most directors allow casting company personnel to run auditions, and they do well, for they do it all the time. It is difficult, but a time schedule should be maintained and ample study materials (e.g., scripts) should be available. ❞

PREPARATIONS AND PROCEDURES

It's been a while since you announced your project to the world. By now you've arranged a suitable place to hold your auditions. (See Chapter Three.) You've received your SAG sign-in sheet and you've created your own sign-in sheet and informational check-in form. You have selected only those actors right for a role to come in and read from the script. You have scheduled appointments, emailed confirmations and let folks know what subway stop or bus to take or where to park and how to get to your location. Finally the day has arrived. You are ready to begin.

In a sense, this first-time meeting with an actor is a callback: you've already reviewed their resume for experience level, you've seen the reel and have a sense of them as a performer, and you know they are right for your project. Something in you says "Yes, that is what I'm looking for." Even though you are now meeting them for the first time, something feels right. You already have a response to this person's work, their energy, how they photograph. So have fun. Trust your gut. Trust your instincts.

Provide scripts in advance.

If you expect actors to do a good job, give them time to prepare. SAG rules require actors to have scripts a minimum of 24 hours in advance. Give them a week. Send the actors a PDF file of the side pages you've created from your master script so they can prepare for their reading with you. Use the PDF setting in your print menu. Do not send your script in your scriptwriting software. If the receiver doesn't have that program, they will have trouble opening the attachment. If they open it in an alternative program, it is likely that all the formatting will be lost. So, use the PDF in your print menu. Another alternative for distributing sides is to put them on your film's website or your group email list serve available for download. Send an email instructing these selected actors to go to your website and download the appropriate character's sides. Creating a Yahoo! or Google group for your project can also streamline your communications.

Make a schedule.

You are ready with your schedule. Names are filled in next to appointments. Give a copy to each staff person with you in the audition space, your DP and your producer. Instruct your gatekeeper to check them off on this sheet as the actors come and go. This is for your records. The SAG sign-in sheet is for the SAG office. SAG has to know whether you run your sessions on time. When casting a big-budget commercial, if you run late, there are fines and paid wait time. It's rare, but it happens.

Setting up.

You need a reception area with access to restrooms. Your reception area is indicative of your level of professionalism. Set up a table for your sign-in sheets: one for SAG members and one for non-union actors. (Yes, non-union actors can work alongside union actors, but you have to keep the sign-in sheets separate.) Have extra pens, paper, a stapler for headshots and resumes. Actors know to bring a hard copy of their headshot and resume to the audition, but be sure to have mentioned it anyway in the confirmation email you sent out last week.

Allow enough time for each actor.

Avoid overbooking your schedule. If you want actors to do a short monologue in addition to reading a scene from the script, you are going to need around 8 to 10 minutes per person to get each person in the room, do the monologue, read the script, take some direction from you, and go again. Spending 10 minutes now can save a wasted callback. It helps you be really sure of your choices. Do the math for 10 minutes with each actor: six actors per hour. Schedule a break every two hours, and a lunch break in the middle. This will give you time to catch your breath if you get backed up and are running late. Don't make the mistake of not building breaks into the schedule.

INFORMATION FORM

When an actor arrives, they will "check in" by signing in on the sign-in sheet. Another form to consider is an informational form filled out upon arrival to the audition. It's an easy way to collect any other information you need, such as direct phone numbers, when actors only have agents and managers on the resume. More importantly, it is a way for actors to let you know schedule conflicts. If they have a television series shooting weekdays, but want to work a supporting role in your film, they can let you know which weekends work best. If they have a comedy club gig on Saturday nights, they can let you know they would need to wrap by early evening.

Keep secrets.

It's a good idea to keep audition locations private by telling only those actors chosen to come in for a read exactly where the audition is going to be held. The exception would be an open call where it is announced that actors may come anytime between certain hours at a specified location.

We keep location information secret to avoid gatecrashers. Some idiot is going to try to get in anyway. On a feature I was recently casting, an actor found out where the auditions were being held and managed to talk his way past the gatekeeper. Another actor who *was* selected gave a friend the audition location. The friend managed to waste his own time getting there, as well as the director's time in dealing with the situation. He didn't have an appointment and was already in the reject pile, because we already had prescreened actors' headshots, reels and resumes.

HOW MANY ACTORS DO I SEE FOR EACH ROLE?

If you carefully prescreen submission materials, avoid gratuitous auditions of your friends and those who just want the audition experience, you will hopefully have reduced the "Yes" pile to less than 10 to 15 actors per role for supporting roles. If you find yourself with many more, ask yourself: Are you really clear in your mind how you see each character? Do you fully understand the character traits intrinsic in each character type? Review the resume for experience level. Get really specific with how you see each character. Only see actors who truly meet this vision.

WHO DO I CAST FIRST?

Cast your leading actors first.

Your leading actors are essential to have in place. Take your time, and be sure of your final decision. Sleep on it before making your offer. The two or three of you are going to be spending a lot of time together. Remember the camping story? This is a good time to test the theory. (See this book's preface by Robert Pickett.)

For your leading actors, see as many actors as you have time for who you truly see in the part. After your leads are signed, sealed and delivered in writing, get going on the supporting roles. Most likely you started searching and posting at the same time, but your focus has been on your leading actors.

Listen to your gut, follow your instincts and keep looking until it hits you: "Yes! That's the person I want in my movie!" And it will — in a moment, in a flash. Someone will walk into the room and you will suddenly perk up, feel inspired, and perhaps relieved to find another potential.

Try to avoid reading anyone for a lead with less than five or six major supporting roles in other films. If they don't have any leading roles yet, and this is their first, be sure they're really ready to take on the demands of a leading role. Be sure this person really can "carry" your film. By "carry" your film, we mean they will not only get the job done, but also turn in a complete performance, and be someone the audience will want to watch for your 90 to 120 pages. Leading actors are able to fulfill the demands of the character's journey and hold the audience's interest throughout the entire movie.

Remember, you have what they want: a leading role in a feature film. You can keep looking. There are plenty of fish in the sea.

Supporting actors.

As you read the supporting roles against your choices for leads (in callbacks) you will be looking for that mysterious thing called "chemistry." During this first round your job is to create a list with several possibilities for each of the supporting roles. It will come down to scheduling and availability when it's time to make offers. I recommend first, second and third choices for each role.

Background extras.

You will be way too busy to be thinking about background extras. Hire someone or assign this to your assistant director. Your AD will be responsible for filling the background casting position. You will need to think about how many, if any, for all your locations, and you need to put this on your production meeting agenda. Remember to add total headcounts to your catering schedule to feed people. The more people on-set, the longer it takes to get through setups. Concentrate your shooting schedule and move your extras through setup and wardrobe changes to get the most out of your day. You're moving people and equipment and you need to pay attention to how you schedule extras. Don't forget additional bathrooms.

INSIDE THE SESSION

Control the room.

This actor has been waiting to come in and frequently may be somewhat nervous. It is your job to help them feel at ease and keep the mood in the room relaxed.

Have your gatekeeper/host bring actors in one at a time, say their name, hand you their headshot and casting form if you are using one. Casting forms can be icebreakers. What needs to happen next depends on whether you run the room or a "room host" runs the room. This person is the first one to speak. Welcome the actor. Take a moment to introduce anyone else in the room, find a way to connect. Ask a few questions. Show interest. Tell them what's going to happen next, whether to do the monologue and then read from the script, or jump right in with the script reading. Or maybe you want to start with some improvisation.

Casting sessions are job interviews.

For anyone to do well under the stress of a job interview requires preparation. Auditions are nerve-wracking. Let it be okay for an actor to start material over. Put actors at ease and create a pleasant place to do the audition. Instruct your staff to remain calm. All workplace rules apply: no disrespectful behavior; no harassment, sexual or otherwise.

Casting sessions are private.

Actors up for the same role do not watch each other's auditions. It is standard practice to see people one at a time for the first session. Focus on each actor for each role one at a time. You'll bring them back to read with other actors to test chemistry in the callback sessions. For now it's one at a time. The only decision for now is whether you want to see them again. It's just one layer of the filtering and decision process. Trust the process. You aren't making final decisions right now.

Memorized sides.

The best actors are usually the best prepared. Most actors are going to want to memorize sides so they can work on character, relationship and emotional states. Memorization frees the actor to create character. They may or may not hold onto the script for reference. It is a job interview and you can expect an actor to glance down at the script even if they do have it memorized.

Using a reader.

Have someone in the room to read the script with the actor. They sit or stand opposite the actor, usually with their back to the camera. The director sits center at the table with the producer(s) and anyone else who needs to be in the casting session. The actor stands in front of the table, framed medium to close by the camera operator who has set up the camera and the end of the table. The reader sits between the camera and the actor, out of frame line, or over the shoulder if the scene is done standing. Have a chair available. See Figure 4.

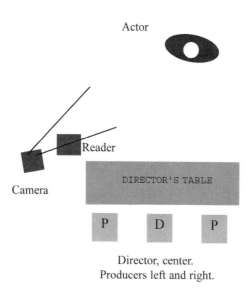

Director, center.
Producers left and right.

Figure 4: Room Set-Up with Camera.

Recording the casting session.

The purpose of recording your sessions is strictly to help you recall what the actors did for you. It is a reminder. It doesn't have to be perfect footage. You don't need to have a perfect three-point light setup. It's a simple way of keeping track of actors and knowing what they look like in close-up. Also, it can be very telling of an actor's level of "on-camera" readiness.

Do they know how to play angles?

Do they know how to play a close-up versus a medium or wide shot?

Are they "camera-ready" for a lead?

Can they match any action?

Remember to check sound levels. Hang a microphone overhead, or if you are close enough, use the on-board microphone on your camera, which is going to be just fine for a reading. Clip-on mics, which are going to pick up clothing and paper noise close to the body, are a waste of time.

Have your camera operator compose a medium shot on the actor reading and stay off the reader. Instruct your camera operator to go in for a CU, close-up shot somewhere during the reading.

Adjustments and direction when
you have something to say.

Test the waters. Give adjustments to actors you are interested in seeing more from. Or just put them in the "Callback" pile if you're pressed for time. Try not to keep people waiting. You did, after all, set appointments. Remember that this is just the first round of auditions. You need to keep things moving, and now may not be the time to take 20 minutes with one actor and stall the schedule. If you know you love them in the role, it will be enough to put them in the "Callback" pile and keep moving.

If you are unsure how much someone piques your interest, have him or her read the scene again. Be specific with your direction. Vague directions lead to vague results and wasted time and you won't see what you need to make the best casting decisions. Give actors things to do. Avoid giving directions that include telling actors how they're supposed to feel. Feeling an emotion is a result, a reaction. When you change the action — what they are doing — the emotional content also will change.

How you FEEL (emotional content/connection) is a *result* of what you do (action). Actors respond to *doing things* (feeling comes from doing), as in doing a physical activity such as making a sandwich, sorting the mail, folding the laundry, shopping for groceries, etc. A good actor is *doing* the right action for the desired emotional outcome. Avoid telling actors *how* to feel or *what* to feel. It is their job to give you an action that produces the desired emotional result. Professional actors know how to give you the emotional content you want, which should be evident in the text. That is their job.

You wouldn't tell your DP how to run his equipment. Don't do it with actors. If none of this makes sense to you, then you may not be ready to direct professional actors. Directing is a fine art and requires skill, leadership, communication and finesse. See Chapter Five for a bigger discussion on working with actors.

MORE BASIC DOs AND DON'Ts

Do expect actors to be prepared and on time.
No one likes to be late for appointments. Assume positive intent with people. Be patient when there are traffic jams and forgiving if people arrive a few minutes late. Have someone else go ahead. Anyone running late is probably freaking out trying to get to you. So, be kind. It won't hurt.

Do expect actors to arrive with a headshot and a resume.

Arriving with headshots and resumes is standard procedure, but it doesn't hurt to add a reminder in the confirmation email. For new actors without a formal headshot submitting for "Day Player" or "walk-on" roles, request that they bring a recent snapshot. Actors just starting out may not have invested in expensive headshots yet. But they might put their heart into a bit part.

Nudity, scars and tattoos.

Never ask actors to remove clothing at an audition. Even when there is nudity, you don't do it at the audition. When the time comes you will need a person of the same sex as the actor doing the nudity in the room, and the actor who is doing the nudity should be free to bring someone with them. Because you listed the nudity in the breakdown, anyone on your list for this role is already aware of the nudity. Expect to be asked about the necessity of the nudity, and to provide an approximate shot list.

If you have scenes in a shower or bath, or in bathing suits, ask about scars or tattoos you wouldn't want the camera to see. There are assorted makeup products to cover them up if necessary.

Be sure that somewhere in the session you ask them if they have read the breakdown and are fully aware of the nudity. Ask them if they have any questions about the nudity.

Don't ask actors to sign a release form for audition footage.

Audition footage is just that: audition footage. It is not a final product and you don't have the right to use it anywhere in your movie or post to a website, or sell to the paparazzi. Releases are signed when contracts are turned in. It is part of the standard preproduction paperwork to have releases for all of your actors. Because the audition is not a shoot date, you don't need a release of rights for audition footage. No one but you is going to see the audition footage. Actors do not give away audition footage rights, and it is not yours to take. You don't have rights to audition footage.

Keep an open mind to all potential and opportunity.
Remember to focus, take your time and have fun. If you exude an enthusiasm while staying relaxed, it will help your actors focus and relax as well. Everyone wants to do well in auditions. Remember you are not making any final decisions.

Ending the session.
If you think you know before the actor finishes the scene that they're not right for the role, be certain before you send them on their way. Give them a chance. Offer a suggestion and hear the scene again. They might surprise you. Thank them for coming in, and discreetly mark your spreadsheet in the callback column — "Yes" or "No." Place their headshot in either the "Callback" pile or "No Callback" pile. Then move on to the next actor.

We all know it takes time to get back to people, so no one expects to know right away. It's polite, however, and therefore good practice, to let people know whether it will be a few days or a few weeks. Try to get back via email to everyone you've met. It's rude to leave people wondering. They took the time to come in to see you. You can take a moment and follow-up with them. See Chapter Eight for more on how to handle rejections.

Keep track.
Make a few notes on your audition schedule or on the back of the headshot, or on the audition form, if you're using one. A few things to keep in mind include:

How were they at taking your direction?

Did you feel a connection?

Did they listen to you?

Did you see anything different from the first reading to the last?

If you have time, and you probably won't, you might ask if they have any questions. Most experienced actors will keep it short, and know that you can't discuss callbacks. If you do, be prepared for things like:

When are you shooting? Again, it is best to phrase in generalities. Things change. Locations get lost, actors drop off the radar. Things will happen that delay shooting.

When are the callbacks? Avoid specifics. "We'll let you know" or "We're not sure, but within a few weeks" is professional and safe. You don't want to say "This Thursday and Friday" and then have that actor not make the list. You'd be surprised what actors have done to crash the party.

Can I crew and do a part for you? It is not all that uncommon, especially in non-union projects, for an actor to also serve as a crew member.

Sorting the session: Do you need more options?

During the first round your task is to consider who is in your "Yes" pile for a callback, and who is in your "No" pile. If the "Yes" pile is too lean, and you feel you need more choices, it is important to pay attention to this hunch. If you think you need to see more options, then see more actors. Don't delay. It's a sign that you haven't seen what you're looking for, what you see in your head.

Search further and repeat the first audition round process. You may have to increase your market range. You may need to dig into your referrals and see who friends can recommend. You can reach out to teachers and colleagues. You can post to your social networking sites.

Let us move on to callbacks.

CHAPTER TEN

THE SECOND ROUND —
CALLBACKS

"All I try to do is create an atmosphere that seems comfortable enough, that it removes tension and everyone feels free. If they feel free then behavior happens, small moments happen, and that's what ultimately works the best for me." — BARRY LEVINSON

CONFIRMING YOUR CHOICES

By now you have completed a few days of first-round auditions. Next is to review the stacks of headshots and the audition footage and see who to "call back." Sometimes callbacks are right away, perhaps at the end of the same week. Sometimes you will want to take a few weeks. You may have to meet with producers or other people on your team who have a say in the casting choices.

During the first round, you had a gut response to an actor. Notice how you were engaged and interested, or distracted and found them to be unsuited. You made notes on the back of the headshots or the audition form. (Remember to destroy these notes and don't let anyone break confidentiality.) Take some time to review all of this. Now turn on the playback and watch the footage. Are your initial instincts the same? Are you now noticing that there is something about them you find annoying? Do you like one over another even more?

Next, sort everyone into "Callback For Sure" and "Callback Maybe" piles. Anyone in the "No Callback" pile will need to be sent an appropriate email. Keep it polite and professional. Here's a suggestion:

Dear _____,

Thank you so much for coming in on _____ to read for us. We appreciate your time. We are now moving on with Callbacks and are sorry to inform you we cannot offer you an appointment at this time. You're a great actor, just not what we're looking for in the role. We wish you all the best with your endeavors.

Regards,

Casting Team — (PROJECT TITLE)

CALLBACK FOR SURE

The "Callback For Sure" pile is reserved for those actors you need to see more of, or actors you can fully see playing the role: actors it could be fine to make an offer to. Another actor in the "Callback Maybe" pile might do something surprising and become your first choice. You will know for sure when you know for certain. You may even have three or four choices for each role that delight you. Consider yourself lucky when this happens. You still don't have to make a final decision yet. Allow yourself time to go through the process. You might change your mind.

When you have your completed "Callback For Sure" pile, it is time to make a phone call. Contact the actor. Do not leave details on voice mail. Keep it short and save the details for the actual phone conversation:

"Hi (Actor),

This is Jane Doe, the director on (PROJECT TITLE). I would like to speak with you about a Callback as soon as possible. Please call me at (YOUR NUMBER) when you get a moment. Thanks for auditioning. We really enjoyed meeting you. The best time to reach me is (TIME)."

Avoid receiving long voicemail messages along with the risk of losing someone in the numerous messages you have, but do include this:

"Please, if your call rolls over to voicemail, do not leave a message, simply call me later."

Because you have what they want, actors will call you back fairly soon. If you don't hear from someone within a reasonable amount of time, and in this case less than 24 hours, you need to call again. Perhaps your message was lost. Don't take chances. Call again. When you connect, offer a few schedule options and a few clear and simple suggestions of what you would like to see them prepare at the callback. If there is a new scene to read, let them know it will be emailed as before. Or send them to your website to download the file.

Then, and this is crucial: Ask if they have any questions for you. Create a great beginning to a good working relationship based on clear communication, respect and professionalism.

CALLBACK MAYBE

The "Callback Maybe" pile is for those who you can see in the role, but you like your other choices better. This is your secondary callback schedule list, and can be done via email. Of course, if you want to do this pile by phone, go for it, but email will be fine. (Don't let your "Maybe" pile distract you from contacting your "For Sure" pile quickly.)

Dear_____,

We enjoyed meeting you at our auditions for (PROJECT TITLE). Please send us two possible audition times on (DAY, DATE, TIME) for a Callback. An additional script is attached to this email. We look forward to hearing from you and will confirm your appointment.

Again, thanks for your interest in our movie. We look forward to hearing from you.

Regards,

Director/Casting Team, (PROJECT TITLE)

PROCEDURES

Repeat the steps from your first round of auditions: book your audition space and have your audition team ready (gatekeeper, camera operator, reader, etc.).

Set callback appointments.

Allow more time with callbacks. For major supporting roles, especially if you are reading them with someone you have already cast, 20 to 30 minutes is about right. Expect to take more time with leading roles, even an hour. You must be especially confident with your leading roles. Set appointments accordingly.

It is acceptable to have several rounds of callbacks. Actors are used to coming in repeatedly. They understand the process and go through it frequently. I mention this because several early career directors I've worked with were very nervous about having actors come back twice and felt we were abusing our time with them. Let that go. It's all part of the day's business.

Test your communication and directing approach.

Have the actor read what they have prepared, and then you dive in and make suggestions. In other words, you want to test whether this actor understands how you give direction. Some actors respond to "do it this way, like this," and some actors detest this approach. Some actors respond better with the "try this and see what happens" approach. Because actors need and want to be included in the process of how the scene will play, ask if they have anything else they want to try before ending the session. Take a few minutes now to test the waters with someone you may be spending 12 to 14 hours a day with.

Put on your "poker face."

Avoid rolling your eyes in disbelief when something comes out truly awful. It's tacky and rude. You may or may not hear or see any difference in the reading, but you must always respond with a positive comment. Keep it respectful and professional. When you know for sure you've seen enough, say something generic:

"Great. Okay. That's terrific. I'm good. Thank you for coming in."

Sleep on your decisions.

Never make an offer during the session. You want to be sure. You may need to review choices with your staff. When you are ready to make an offer, it's time for a phone call.

There really is no reason casting sessions have to be painful. Trust the process and understand that actors do this all the time and want to do their best because they want to land the roles. They look forward to trying various ways of playing the scene. They are eager to listen to your ideas. They work hard to get it right and be "The One." Everyone wants to be "The One."

CHAPTER ELEVEN

OFFERS AND CONTRACTS

"I ain't no actor. I'm a star. Actors can become stars, but there are damn few stars that become actors." — BUFFALO BILL CODY in THE WILD WEST SHOW, Chicago

Get it in writing. Oh, such famous words. *Just Do It.* More famous words. *Fools Die Hard.* Learn from your mistakes and listen to the advice of people who know more than you do: Write up your agreements, even with your friends.

If you are spending OPM (other people's money) to make this movie, someone on your team — you perhaps — will be held accountable for financial transactions. Whether union or non-union, you will want to have a written agreement in place. It should cover the basics: said actor is obligated to shoot this character on these dates for this amount of money, or in exchange for screen credit, meals, etc. Actors will want to see something about the length of the days. Twelve-hour days are long enough. On extremely long days, you run the risk of accidents when people get tired. (Be sure you have production insurance.) You may want an indemnity clause and many will want a confidentiality clause, common when "A-listers" are on-set. If you are renting equipment, the rental house will need your insurance policy number.

A simple Internet search will guide you to the appropriate forms. Check for movie budgeting software that includes contract templates. Or check out free legal documents here: *free-legal-document.com.*

When working on a no-pay project, it is equally important to state when actors will get the copy of their footage. Think of it as a form of pay. You need to honor that obligation. They need the footage for their demo reels, the major reason they are agreeing to be in your movie and work for no pay. Waiting until you get out of postproduction is too long to wait for clips.

Be sure your editor understands that actors will need clips as soon as possible after their characters wrap. It is the chief complaint actors have when working on non-union, low-budget projects: In the audition breakdown they were told there would be "copy, credit and meals," and the copy never comes, the meals are a joke, and the screen credit misspelled a name.

In general, it shouldn't cost actors money to be in a project that doesn't pay money. You need to include reimbursements for parking or public transit, gas and bridge tolls, makeup and dry cleaning if they use their own clothing. It's the right thing to do.

UNION CONTRACTS

SAG requires a number of forms. Most of these forms have already been mentioned and are typically completed prior to casting. It is prudent to hire a line producer or an associate producer with experience handling the paper flow. There are several contracts to choose from: Standard, Low-budget, Modified Low-budget, Ultra Low-budget, Experimental, Limited Distribution, Deferred Pay, Student, and others.

Which contract you qualify for depends on several things — primarily your budget and your distribution plan. You can't pay an "A-list" actor millions, and everyone else Ultra

Low-budget. There are things such as fair labor practices to consider. To qualify for the student contract, you must be enrolled in school and provide appropriate documentation. Visit *sag.org* and read the various contracts to determine which one suits your project the best.

Pay attention to "Local Hires Only" clauses. LHO is when actors are contracted from the local jurisdiction. For example, if you are shooting in Chicago, any actors on your picture not from Chicago Local will need to be paid travel and a *per diem*. No longer can Los Angeles-based actors come to San Francisco and climb onboard as a local hire, which used to happen frequently by way of actors staying with friends to avoid a hotel bill. Since SAG actors have to be current with their dues to be eligible to work on a union shoot, you will be checking status with their SAG member number. Understand that there are no restrictions on who you hire as long as they are paid-up active members. When you bring someone from New York for a lead to your location in New Orleans, just follow the rules: coming from another local, you will have to pay travel expenses, hotel and a *per diem*. It's a job site. If you bring in actors from another city and don't pay the travel and hotel, you risk contract violations and fines. See Chapter Three for more on the decision to work with the actors' unions.

Consider hiring actors for leads and major supporting roles in New York City or Los Angeles with really great experience, actors who can help your film get the attention it deserves. Then hire smaller supporting roles and bit parts locally. If you are shooting in New Orleans, hire supporting actors from New Orleans. If your lead actor is from New York, include the travel, hotel and a *per diem* in your cost analysis for talent. Up-and-coming actors with great credits are hungry for good roles in features. They can help you tremendously when applying to the film festivals.

There are many ways to work with professionals on very low budgets. There are exceptions to SAG rules, such as actors who are on "Financial Core" and are eligible to work on non-union projects. It is worth your time to understand exactly what this is. It allows union actors to work on really low-budget films with non-union crew. Read the details of the Experimental and Modified Low-budget agreements.

CHAPTER TWELVE

DON'T TAKE MY WORD FOR IT — FRIENDS CHIME IN

"If there's specific resistance to women making movies, I just choose to ignore that as an obstacle for two reasons: I can't change my gender, and I refuse to stop making movies." — KATHRYN BIGELOW

FAST, CHEAP, GOOD — PICK TWO

Fast. Cheap. Good. You can only have two. Some of the best advice I ever heard is the rule of three. Here we see it applied to moviemaking as well. Let's break it down:

FAST and CHEAP? Forget it. Not possible. Fast AND cheap is just no good. Fast and cheap is crap. Fast and cheap is going to be fraught with bad choices. People get hurt. Careers are ruined. No one wants to waste time on another poorly made film.

FAST and GOOD? Only if you can spend more money. Fast AND good ain't cheap. Fast and good is going to cost more money. You'll need the best of the best to get it done fast and good, and they're expensive.

Which leaves most of us with:

CHEAP and GOOD? Only if there is more time. Cheap AND good ain't fast. It takes more time. If you don't have a lot of money to spend, then you need to take your time and get it right. Experienced people can, and do, get more done in less time. Sure, it is possible to work fast and have a good end product, but it's going to cost you more time, better equipment, and better people.

A LITTLE HELP FROM OUR FRIENDS

Actors do a shout out.

What's the worst thing you saw in any audition process, besides running late?

As I waited to read, I overheard the casting director on the phone making a deal for another actor to get the role I was reading for. When he called me in to read, he never even looked at me, rushed me and said, "Thank you and good-bye". Totally wasted my time.

■ ■ ■ ■ ■

I think it must have been the location. We met in a park because the shoot was exterior. That was my first clue that this guy didn't have a clue. I never should have agreed to show up.

■ ■ ■ ■ ■

Having the cute pre-teen daughter/son/niece/nephew of the producer/director/cameraperson be the reader in a scene with me. Not only do they have difficulty reading the text, they have no idea what they are saying. This has happened a few times to me — more recently she was 11, and once it was a 9-year-old.

■ ■ ■ ■ ■

The worst thing in any audition process is to show overt preference for someone who is auditioning. This irritates everyone who notices it. Most directors allow casting company personnel to run auditions and they do well, for they do it all the time. It is difficult, but a time schedule should be maintained and ample study materials (e.g., scripts) should be available.

■ ■ ■ ■ ■

Smoking in the audition room: Just before I went in to sing they had been smoking. The small room was filled with smoke.

■ ■ ■ ■ ■

Directorial Humiliation: Rather than responding to my character, rather than attempting to "give" on an organic level, the casting director chose to parody (out of embarrassment perhaps?) the scene, and to destroy the moment for me, and, it appeared, for the producer who was also present in the room. It was, I felt, really disrespectful and unprofessional. So when the casting director provides a hindrance for the very session which they arranged, to serve the needs of the client/producer, and find an actor they are searching for, then the deck is stacked even higher against the actor. We don't need any more odds against us, do we? I really don't think so.

■ ■ ■ ■ ■

I was asked if I wouldn't mind driving 12 hours to audition at a secret location in Vermont. It was an intimate scene with two award-winning "A-list" actors. I did it. I got a call three days later to hold the date, and was told "Director loved the tape." They even gave me a phone number. After patiently waiting two weeks I used the number only to find it was disconnected. They had abruptly closed shop and moved the location back to Hollywood without informing anyone. Just let people know what's going on. We just want to know what's going on.

■ ■ ■ ■ ■

My all-time favorite irksome thing at a casting is when an actor is asked to do improvisation in the audition and then, after the actor leaves, the casting director gives that actor's improvisations as direction to the actors that audition after them. Instead of the client seeing the unique improvisations that the first actor brought to the audition, they see every actor doing the same thing. This cuts the legs out from under the first actor.

■ ■ ■ ■ ■

Clients who use the improvisations of one actor in a commercial audition but hire another actor to use those improvisations. It's happened to me several times with both on-camera improvisation auditions and when I've used a unique character voice in a radio voiceover audition.

■ ■ ■ ■ ■

Being asked to perform every scene five or six times for one of two roles in an industrial film — the audition lasted over two hours.

■ ■ ■ ■ ■

I spent time in Europe (Thank you, Uncle Sam!) and spent time with Europeans, so got very good at mimicry of foreign accents. I attempted to pass myself off as being from the UK when a voiceover production house sought authentic English accents. It turns out the CEO was from England. I got caught with my accent down!

What's the nuttiest thing you ever did to land a part?

Bold, not too nutty though: Saw an ad in The Hollywood Reporter *promoting a film project. The film seemed right for me, so I sent a letter to the director/ writer telling him how I would be an asset to his film and he called me in for a meeting. He ended up giving me a part and expanded the role for me. I was off to Israel for three months of fun work and great experiences.*

What advice do you have for directors to do a better job running auditions?

Know what you're looking for and don't waste people's time. As much as I may want to feel like a director really saw me, I don't want to be humored or have to jump through any hoops unnecessarily. How an actor feels leaving an audition is based solely on your reactions to what they do, not on what you have them do.

■ ■ ■ ■ ■

Be specific as to what they want you to prepare at the audition and ask for adjustments at the reading. If the role is pre-cast, tell the actors.

■ ■ ■ ■ ■

Get there early. I've seen so many directors stroll in late. We wonder why things are behind at 4 p.m. — because they've been behind since the day started.

■ ■ ■ ■ ■

Take a few moments with actors to make them feel welcome. If the first read is not great, allow a do-over with solid direction and suggestions. Follow-up feedback is like gold to actors, so much appreciated but rarely given.

■ ■ ■ ■ ■

It's so important to run on time. I left to feed my parking meter after an hour and the person running the auditions called for me while I was out. He didn't let me go in next. He was rude. So I left. I never did get to meet the director.

■ ■ ■ ■ ■

PRIOR to an audition, send out as much info as possible — projected shoot start dates, how many shoots dates are needed for the character I am auditioning for, where you're shooting, etc. Are you providing makeup, hair, wardrobe and meals? It saves time and shows me you're organized.

■ ■ ■ ■ ■

It would be nice if I can read a script or detailed synopsis BEFORE I audition so I won't waste my time or yours if I realize this is not a story for me to tell. Let us know beforehand if you want a monologue or cold read and what to expect when we walk in.

■ ■ ■ ■ ■

If you're running late, please have someone come out and acknowledge it.
Just communicate and show your respect for our time. Please hold auditions
somewhere that's easy to access. Provide water and snacks in the waiting area.
Whether or not I eat or drink anything, I always feel that those who do that will
also take care of me on-set.

■ ■ ■ ■ ■

Be organized! Be professional! Have sides printed out. Don't expect us to always
have ours printed. I usually do but I may not have all the sides. Have someone
greet us to check us in.

■ ■ ■ ■ ■

Keep it short, but not too short. I like to spend at least 10 to 15 minutes (no
more than 30 minutes) in the room so we all get a sense of each other. I am
auditioning you as well. Do I want to spend X amount of days on a set with
you? Do I feel I can trust you and feel safe as an actor to really open up and
give my best performance with you?

What's the most fabulous thing a director did to help you succeed at an audition, or, apart from being right for a role, how did you land the role over the others who were also right for the role?

They smiled at my joke and assured me I could relax. Instantly, that's what I did.

■ ■ ■ ■ ■

The director put me in front of a bronze statue in South Station Boston and
asked me to pretend I was a tour director in a museum. He wanted me to "riff"
on the statue. I was making up some ridiculous stuff! But the key was that I
made him believe me. It got me a role in a commercial that paid handsomely.

■ ■ ■ ■ ■

To let me know what he was looking for before I did anything. He asked me
some questions to get to know me and paid attention when I auditioned and
seemed to care that I was there. Respect and consideration go a long way.

■ ■ ■ ■ ■

Any director that lets you make adjustments and try the piece again in a differ-
ent way is giving you the opportunity to give your best.

■ ■ ■ ■ ■

There was a part I was right for but was written for a man. My manager
convinced the director and producer to consider reading me. Thanks to them
being open-minded, I was invited to read. I was the only woman considered. I
had three callbacks and each time they took their time, really listened to my

readings, gave lots of direction and allowed me to expand my performance each time. I won the co-starring feature role.

■ ■ ■ ■ ■

He really coached me. He knew how to direct actors. He communicated well and it felt like a mini coaching session rather than an audition.

Apart from being right for a role, how did YOU land the role over the others who were also right for the role?

By asking the director of the commercial a single question at the callback. The director says, "Gee, I don't know. Lets try it both ways!" I did two very different takes and learned I had landed the role an hour after I left the office.

■ ■ ■ ■ ■

I made eye contact with the director and had a good connection, personality-wise.

■ ■ ■ ■ ■

I brought something extra to the audition. I have no idea what it was. Probably something different in each case that the director saw and felt made me the right fit.

■ ■ ■ ■ ■

Nine times out of 10, the director has no idea what she/he wants until it walks in the door. If he knows, he already has someone in mind. If he doesn't, he won't know until it hits him in the face.

■ ■ ■ ■ ■

I stayed in touch with the director afterwards, thanked him for his time, and said I really enjoyed meeting him, regardless of his decision to please keep me in his loop. And yes, it was all true. I wasn't buttering them up!

■ ■ ■ ■ ■

I wore a giant red bra with huge tassels under a shawl and carried my trumpet in a case on stage to audition for "Mazeppa" the stripper in Gypsy. *When I got on stage I flipped off the shawl, opened the case and pulled out my trumpet. Of course, I performed "You Gotta Have A Gimmick," complete with bent-over/ trumpet-between-the-legs routine, for the director and her staff. They were laughing so hard I think they peed their pants. This was a huge risk but it worked. It is still one of my favorite roles I ever played.*

■ ■ ■ ■ ■

The nuttiest thing I ever did to land a part was to dress like a fisherman for a seafood commercial. The actor who landed the job was dressed exactly like the fisherman on the label and he got the job and probably still has it. So, it's not nutty, but smart.

■ ■ ■ ■ ■

On one audition for an anti-violence Public Service Announcement for hockey, the director asked me what I did and when I told him I was a hockey coach, a real one, I got the job immediately. There were others equally talented as actors, but none were the real deal.

Directors do a shout out.

What's the nuttiest thing you ever saw an actor do in an audition?

Lie on a resume or really stretch the truth. If a show's title ends with the words "On Ice," then it is not a Broadway national tour. We know.

■ ■ ■ ■ ■

Actors who worry too much about what the client may want instead of focusing on what they as an actor have to uniquely bring to the piece.

■ ■ ■ ■ ■

The actor pulled a giant boa constrictor out of a bag and draped it around himself as part of his monologue. Our production stage manager had a snake phobia and left the room, very upset. The actor was not cast.

■ ■ ■ ■ ■

It's hard to pick "the nuttiest" thing I've seen an actor do because as a director, you see some pretty horrible things in an audition. People will come in to sing for you, even if they genuinely cannot sing. I had to choke down laughter when one girl came in with 32 bars of "Part Of Your World" from The Little Mermaid. *I had only asked for 16 bars, but her rendition was so horrible and comedic, I couldn't even stop it at 16 bars because if I opened my mouth, I would have burst out laughing. Another actor sang "Stars" from* Les Misérables *while walking around the room maniacally, singing each line to a different direction of the compass while sawing his arms about the air. Unreal. It's always good to have an honest friend, which is more rare than you might think, but find that friend who will tell you how awful you are and be brave enough to show them what you have before you go into an audition, because the last thing you want is to go in and do that horrible thing in front of the director. People might not like Simon from* American Idol, *but he is both honest and realistic, and while people might not like how he puts other people down, he is to be commended for trying to prevent them from ever embarrassing himself like that again. An artist MUST have an accurate self-perception, or they have no hope of any artistic career, ever.*

■ ■ ■ ■ ■

What advice do you have for actors to do better?

Actors who lie about a skill that costs the production time and money when they get to set. Actors who lie about being a principal in a film when they were only an extra, and then getting caught in an audition when they find out that they are auditioning for the person who cast the principals.

■ ■ ■ ■ ■

Learn the appropriate protocol for auditions and follow it. Always.

■ ■ ■ ■ ■

Show confidence. Be friendly. Arrive on time and showed respect.

■ ■ ■ ■ ■

Use material that suits your age and type, no accents, no props, and no graphic sexual stuff.

■ ■ ■ ■ ■

Walk in with confidence, and if you are doing a scripted piece, understand the text. Don't just speak like its rote. Feel it. Confidence, self-esteem and behaving like you already belong in the job will make everyone feel at ease.

■ ■ ■ ■ ■

Never let your nerves get in the way of being the friendliest and nicest person at the audition. Don't overdo it. Directors can spot a phony a mile away. Well, most directors. Always introduce yourself to the support staff. That guy/girl at the table taking your information could have the director's ear and you never know who's talking to whom. Listen. Don't let the other actors get in your space and monopolize your time with chitchat. Focus on the role and the task at hand.

■ ■ ■ ■ ■

What does the character want? Who are they? What/who is my obstacle? Listen. If you are at a cold reading, memorize the first and last line of your sections and the other character's cue lines. If you get your side ahead of time, memorize as much as you can.

■ ■ ■ ■ ■

Network after your audition. Ask yourself pertinent questions.

■ ■ ■ ■ ■

Stay loose and flexible in your concepts — the director may give you another one to deal with. Make a choice and go for it. Listen. Shake hands firmly with as many people as seem open to meeting you. Look them in the eye. SMILE. Listen. Repeat their names. Don't hold your sides up in your face. Let the camera or the director see you. Look up from the side as much as possible. React to the other person reading with you. Listen. Don't worry about reading their lines while you wait for yours. Engage. Be gracious and thank them for the opportunity. Have fun.

■ ■ ■ ■ ■

Clothing: reasonably modest (let me see your body shape but don't have anything tight or revealing), plain colors, no patterns, no excess jewelry, shoes you can walk in easily that support you well (no platforms or highest of high heels), clothes that are flattering and clean, no holes or rips. Not too formal or casual — stay in the middle.

■ ■ ■ ■ ■

If we're asking for monologues, have pieces that are well within the time limit. Keep yourself at least 10 seconds shorter than the maximum.

■ ■ ■ ■ ■

Please be respectful of my very limited time. If you take a lot of time to intro-duce yourself, or amble into the room in a weird mood, or take five minutes to divest yourself of your coat/hat/backpack, etc., or take huge unwarranted pauses in your piece, I absolutely won't cast you, and I'll dislike you to boot.

■ ■ ■ ■ ■

Don't try to "stand out." If you break protocol, you only accomplish looking like a rube and proving to me that you're not professional. Just be a really good actor; then I promise I will remember you.

■ ■ ■ ■ ■

Casting often comes down to the most minute of details. If the leading woman I want most needs to be X inches shorter than our leading man, my decision is almost made for me. Does one actor seem easier to work with? Does one actor have more experience? How much will I have to direct this person? Does this person take direction?

■ ■ ■ ■ ■

Being "right for the role" is how you get the part — ALWAYS — and that doesn't just mean looking and sounding like an archetype for the character you'd be playing. It means that all of the factors a director considers, even the superficial ones, work in your favor, in the subjective opinion of the director. That is what makes you "right" for the role, and that is why you would land it. Casting is 99% of a director's work, and if you have the right cast, most of your job is done. If the director has cast people who were right for the role, the production will be successful, and the majority of people will agree with the casting. Casting your brother's nephew because he is your brother's nephew is obviously one of those factors a director should not be considering, for if your brother's nephew is right for the role because of his familial ties, most people will probably see that, and it will come back to haunt you.

What's the most fabulous thing an actor did to succeed at an audition for you, apart from being right for a role?

They were themselves, allowing me to see who they were, who I'd be working with. They didn't walk in with bravado or a false compensating level of confidence, nor did they look like they were about to die. Happy, but not too happy. The best thing an actor can do at an audition is to be a well-balanced, normal person who I want to work with, someone who cares about how they look (they didn't roll out of bed and are now standing in front of me) and cares what I think about what they are presenting to me.

■ ■ ■ ■ ■

They sang amazingly well.

■ ■ ■ ■ ■

I asked an actor to give me a very still, filmic version of the big bombastic speech he'd just delivered. He asked permission to sit across from me at my table and make eye contact with me, then he delivered the most sincere, connected, authentic speech I've ever seen in audition. I've never forgotten it. He made a huge adjustment in response to my direction. He got the leading role.

■ ■ ■ ■ ■

Personality and reputation: They were open, warm, and professional in person, usually with a good sense of humor. I felt they would be a pleasure to work with. They respected me, enjoyed my direction, knew something about me, and were interested in the project. When I checked with other directors who had worked with them, the response came back 100% positive: low-maintenance, reliable, a good team member, cooperative, creative, disciplined, a positive attitude, consistently friendly with the rest of the cast/crew/staff, no emotional baggage or moodiness, seemed pleased to be with us and freely supportive of the project.

CHAPTER THIRTEEN

CASTING DIRECTORS —
DO YOU NEED ONE?

> "Seventy-five percent of
> directing is casting." —
> ALFRED HITCHCOCK

Whether to hire a casting director depends on many factors. Among them: What are you shooting (feature or commercial, short or voiceover, etc.)? How big is your project? Do you need to tap into the bigger pool of names? You'll find on some projects you know you'll want help, and on other projects, you'll be confident to do it yourself. Here are a few scenarios to consider:

You are about to cast a television commercial (you have a budget to pay standard rates) and you need to shoot in three days, so do you do it yourself, or get help? Every person you bring into your working group creates a new set of deadlines.

You have a three-character movie and you already know your friends (who are trained actors) are going to play these roles. Perhaps you don't need a casting director.

You have some experience with actors and agents, and you are fairly confident that you can run audition sessions and stay on top of communications. Do you go for it? It's a matter of experience and confidence. Consider: Do you know someone you trust who could do a better job than you can? Do you have any experience with it?

Truly, if you don't have a clue, and you're not confident you can follow the instructions in this guide, get a casting director. If you have a huge cast with a large number of background extras shooting over many days, get a casting director. If you need someone to negotiate the finer points of talking to agents because you need a name on your project, get a casting director. If you have more than five or six roles to cast and you need to find actors who will help get your film into the festivals, and you don't know how to find these actors, you'll greatly benefit from a casting director. If you need a lot of background actors for a street scene, or a party, or patrons in a restaurant, you will want to hire someone to wrangle up enough background people for that day's shoot.

The job defined.

Casting directors have a talent for spotting potential. They are resourceful and enjoy the work. They come from a variety of backgrounds: ex-actors, stage directors, crossover agents, personnel directors, and temporary labor managers — all are found throughout the industry. Also, acting teachers and performers do very well as casting directors.

Casting directors fall into two basic categories: background extras or principal casting. Principal casting directors have connections and know how to negotiate contracts, work with unions and contracts, set up paperwork for the production, and handle the entire process.

Background casting can be rough. Background casting directors are fantastic at organizing large groups, mass check-in tables, payroll and tax forms. They are pleasant even under incredible stress, able to handle a walkie-talkie and two egomaniacal actors who forgot they're background, all at the same time. See Chapter Three for more on principal and background casting.

Job tasks and responsibilities:
What will they do for you?

Here is a list of some of the things a casting director will do for you. If you decide not to hire a casting director, these things will still need to get done by someone:

- Organize the breakdown and review character descriptions with the director.
- Create the audition breakdown.
- Distribute the breakdown.
- Follow up on all submissions via phone and email.
- Prescreen all submissions.
- Set up/confirm appointments.
- Secure/provide check-in sheets.
- Book space for your auditions.
- Get scripts to the actors.
- Set up, staff and run the auditions.
- Record the auditions.
- Review the auditions with the director.
- Contact all callbacks.
- Set up the appointments.
- Set up, staff and run the callbacks.
- Contact those selected for callbacks.
- Contact those actors selected for the roles.
- Offer roles, and turn over all contact information to the production office. Sometimes the casting office will check identification and verify work status and distribute/collect IRS forms. At the end of each shoot date, someone will need to complete the payroll vouchers. These are the forms that go to your signatory to cut payroll checks. Generally this responsibility falls to the directing department with 2nd and 3rd assistant directors securing the daily paperwork and pay vouchers.

What's it going to cost?

Some casting directors charge day rates and some a total package that includes all their support staff. Sometimes fees are based on how many roles are to be filled. Fees vary from several hundred dollars a day, averaging three or four days for two or three parts, and up to long-term contracts involving a fee per role. You can negotiate all or some of the standard workflow tasks.

You might wish to have a casting director do the main research and prescreening, while you handle the audition sessions and the videotaping. These are all variables that will determine what you pay and where day rates come in. Day rates typically have "kit fees" added on, such as a daily amount to cover cell phone and office expenses. Another example would be art directors and makeup artists who typically have a day rate plus kit fee. Be sure to ask specific questions when you set out to interview a casting director. With a simple Internet search you will be able to see comparison rates.

Casting directors with "CSA" (Casting Society of America) after their names are most likely the most experienced. The more experience, the more connections to agents and access to known actors. Individuals must be recommended by peers for membership in CSA and have a complete body of work. A casting director with this affiliation will cost you more, but the benefits can certainly outweigh the costs. A recognized casting director can help you land in-demand actors. The relatively known actor is going to help your project get into festivals. As you know, if you are hoping for a distribution deal, film festivals are one route for low-budget Indies. If you already know you are going for direct video Internet sales, then complete unknown actors might work for you and perhaps you won't need a casting director.

Now I can hear you saying, "I can't afford a known actor." Don't make any assumptions about what kind of film this hypothetical known actor is going to say "Yes" to. Actors want to work on great characters in great scripts with great directors making great movies. It's your job to convince them of that to get a "Yes" at the time of contract offer. The proof is going to be in your script. Many great television actors are searching for summer projects while their television series are on hiatus, and they don't really care if they make a lot of money on an Indie film. They want to have a film screened at Sundance, Telluride, Berlin, Toronto or CineQuest, so they can go to a festival and have a good time. Let go of the assumptions about how little an actor will work for go. Remember what I said in the introduction? No more assumptions.

Of course there are many casting directors with great experience who are not CSA members. You can find them by doing a little bit of Internet research. Start at the Screen Actors Guild website (*sag.org*). Look for the pull-down menu in the region you live. Search for the casting directors in that city. Crosscheck credentials at *imdb.com* (The Internet Movie Database) and the Hollywood Creative Directory. A casting director primarily known for big-budget background casting may not be your best choice for principal casting. They're going to be hungry for the principal contract, but be sure they have access to agents, and know where to find great principal actors.

If you're going to use a casting director, use one with experience. It's not an entry-level job for a production assistant. Casting directors are important to have onboard for many reasons: access to agents, posting services, contacts at the union offices. Casting directors know how to find really good actors, and how to handle all the correspondence involved. It is a huge help to have a casting professional on your team. Finding the right actor for a role is a gift, so if you can afford one, do it. Check their credentials and references.

Other resources.

Acting teachers are another great resource for casting. Many are also stage directors, and have inside information on where really good actors in your community are studying. Acting teachers can also help you get the word out to the acting community about your auditions, and make recommendations.

CHAPTER FOURTEEN

SO YOU WANT TO BE A CASTING DIRECTOR

> "Casting is everything. If you get the right people, they make you look good." — TODD SOLONDZ

LOVING ACTORS

Actors are marvelous people: creative, inventive, energetic, positive and fun to be around. If you love working in the entertainment industry and are industrious, efficient, organized, smart about people, understand human chemistry, and enjoy the process of acting, you will have a great time working around directors, actors and casting professionals. Having an appreciation for actors can only help you succeed. Having connections to actors and agents will help too.

You need a director to engage your services, so you will need to network with them. Through various social networking websites you can build an online profile and advertise your services. You will need to register with your regional film resource production guide. In Oregon it's the service resources at Oregon Media Production Association (*ompa.org*), and in Massachusetts post at the Massachusetts Film Office (*mafilm. org*) and *newenglandfilm.com*. In San Francisco, use *reeldirectory.com*. You need to attend networking and screening events where you can meet directors and give them your business card. Attend film festivals and introduce yourself after screenings with directors in attendance. No one can hire you if they can't find you, or don't know who you are.

OUTREACH AND MARKETING

Industry connections.

You must contact agents in the categories of films you wish to cast and build relationships. Visit offices and see who is in their files. Get to know their clientele. Another great way into the industry is to intern.

Getting started.

The busier cities are the better choices for launching a casting business. Outside of New York City and Los Angeles, film has a seasonal fluctuation. Mid-winter in New England is very quiet, while Los Angeles is gearing up for pilot season, the busiest time of the year. You must ask for referrals. Check *mandy.com* and Craigslist and other production crew websites for job postings. Create a website and brand your logo. What makes you different? What can you offer a director over another casting director?

Take any project you can to get started. Volunteer to assist on local features in your community. Consider interning for a good start. You will need recommendations, great connections and referrals. If you are in Los Angeles or New York City, register with the Casting Society of America through their website and sign up as an assistant. Whenever a network or studio CD needs an assistant, this is where they go to find last-minute help. Competition is fierce. Be persistent and keep building your network.

Ken Lazer is a casting director in New York City. Here is what he has to say about getting started in casting:

"I started as an assistant for a casting director that was only supposed to be a two-week trial. Those two weeks turned into four weeks and then after getting a television series, I was asked to stay longer. During the series, we kept getting other film and television projects as well as commercials. We were getting so busy that the casting director had to train me how to run a session with actors. My first session on my own: a "Cool Whip" commercial casting. After the director watched the tapes, he called my boss and said to her, "I've been watching casting sessions for 20 years and this session was the best session I've ever had the pleasure to watch. He's very good. Don't ever let him go." After that phone call, my boss came to me and said, 'You're now in charge of all commercial castings.'"

How important is CSA membership?
"It's not important to me."

How do you set fees? Day rates? Contract for total number of roles?
"It depends on if it's for a television series, feature film or a television commercial. For television/film I consider how many roles there are to cast, the size of the roles to cast (Lead vs. Day Player parts) and how many weeks production is willing to give me to cast all roles. For commercials, I have day rates. There's a prep casting fee and a day casting fee."

What do you like most about working with actors?
"I'm a firm believer in the relationship between casting director and actor. If an actor does a great job at an audition, I look good. So it's important to establish a 'teamwork' type of attitude. I find it rewarding when an actor takes the direction, makes it his/her own, and then ends up getting a callback and/or booking the role."

What advice do you have for film directors to get through the casting process?
"When I get a vague description of the character, I always ask a director when casting a project, "If you could have any celebrity actor play this role, who would it be?" Works every time. After seeing several actors for a particular role on the "first round," it's very important to communicate to the casting director whether or not we're on the right track. Here's a very helpful link: *nyc.gov/html/film/html/index/index.shtml*. A director can find every resource he/she will need and

the City of New York has an incentive program called "Made in NY." With a membership card, vendors offer discounts on their services. Great resource."

Sarah Kliban is a professional actress and casting director specializing in foreign language speakers in the San Francisco Bay Area. Her film casting credits include work on *Milk*, *All About Evil*, *The Kite Runner*, and *The Pursuit of Happyness*. She also teaches classes on auditioning as well as various aspects of the voiceover industry. (Visit her online at *diversitycasting. com*.) Here is what she has to say about how she got started.

How did you get your start in casting?

"I had returned from working in Japan and started working as an actor in San Francisco. At that time, I was fluent both in Japanese and French. My agent called to ask if I would talk to a client directly who needed help casting voices in several different languages. In working with that client, it just made sense that I could specialize in finding foreign-language talent. It all grew from there."

How important is CSA membership to you?

"Being part of a guild is always helpful as there is an exchange of information among colleagues. However, a large number of casting directors are *not* members of CSA. I think this is mainly due to the fact that it is not a union."

How do you set fees? Day rates? Contract for total number of roles?

"My approach to fees is mostly based on the scope of the project. Some of the elements that I look at are: number of roles to cast, number of weeks that we will be casting, difficulty of roles to cast, etc. I use a daily rate for smaller projects and a weekly rate for the longer, extended projects."

What do you like most about working with actors?

"Working with actors is the main reason I work in casting. (The other is problem-solving.) The moments spent in the audition room are the most rewarding: working with the actor directly, reading/performing with them, adjusting their work, generally helping them to achieve their best performance. This is also a very educational experience, both for the actor and for the casting director, getting to know the actor, their strengths and weaknesses, and pushing them forward one audition at a time."

What advice do you have for film directors to get through the casting process?

"Every director sets their own priorities on casting. We can hope the director will be clear as to what they are looking for in a role and also be open to suggestions we make. The casting process does move more slowly than other elements of preproduction. Ideally, the film director can set aside some time to go through the casting process without being too distracted."

What advice do you have for directors of low-budget projects, who may not be able to hire a professional casting director?

"It's *always* better to hire a CD! If you can't find a way to hire a CD to run your casting, you might at least consider hiring a CD for an initial consultation. If that is not possible, the most important thing is to run your auditions as professionally as you can. Try to keep to the schedule, use an environment that is appropriate for auditions, and thank the actors for auditioning."

What are the biggest mistakes directors make when it comes to casting low-budget features?

"Casting people who aren't truly right for the role."

■ ■ ■ ■ ■

And there you have it. When in doubt, always keep looking for the best actors to fit the roles in your projects. Great moviemaking is about making great decisions every step of the way, including your actors.

Years ago, I auditioned to work for a Woody Allen film. The open casting call for background actors brought out hundreds of eligible SAG actors. I recall my number was four hundred and something. When my turn came, I was asked to step up to a line and say hello. Back in the dark under a canopy was Mr. Allen in the flesh, hand-picking every face for every frame, including the background actors. That day on-set was my first day on a big-budget movie. Prior to that, I had worked a few pilot projects and low-budget independent features. That day remains one of the most memorable days in my early career. I will never forget how he hand-picked everyone. It says a lot about a director who takes great care with every aspect of this amazing and wonderful collaboration process.

Good luck, and see you on-set!

GLOSSARY OF COMMON FILM TERMS

These websites helped with the creation of this glossary. They are all excellent online glossary resources.

homepage.newschool.edu/~schlemoj/film_courses/glossary_of_film_terms/glossary.html

allmovie.com/glossary

filmsite.org/filmterms5.html

COMMON TERMS

180-DEGREE RULE — A screen direction rule: an imaginary line on one side of the axis of action is made (e.g., between two principal actors in a scene), and the camera must not cross over that line. To do so results in a visual discontinuity and disorientation; similar to the axis of action (an imaginary line that separates the camera from the action before it) that should not be crossed.

24 FRAMES PER SECOND — Standard frame rate of film speed: the number of frames or images that are projected or displayed per second; in the silent era before a standard was set, many films were projected at 16 or 18 frames per second, but that rate proved to be too slow when attempting to record optical film soundtracks; aka 24fps or 24p.

3-D — Three-dimensional, stereoscopic form or appearance, giving the lifelike illusion of depth; often achieved by viewers donning special red/blue (or green) or polarized lens glasses;

when 3-D images are made interactive so that users feel involved with the scene, the experience is called virtual reality; 3-D experienced a heyday in the early 1950s; aka 3D, three-D, Stereoscopic 3D, Natural Vision 3D, or three-dimensional.

A

ABBY SINGER — The second-to-last shot of the day. Named after production manager Abby Singer, who would frequently call "last shot of the day" or "this shot, and just one more," only to have the director ask for more takes. See also *Martini Shot*.

ABOVE-THE-LINE EXPENSES — The major expenses committed before production begins, including story/rights/continuity (writing); salaries for producers, director and cast; travel and living; and production fees (if the project is bought from an earlier company). Everything else falls under below-the-line expenses. Above-the-line covers costs associated with major creative talent: the stars, the director, the producer(s) and the writer(s), although films with expensive special effects (and few stars) have more above the line budget costs for technical aspects; the term's opposite is *Below the Line*.

ABSTRACT (FORM) — Rejects traditional narrative in favor of using poetic form (color, motion, sound, irrational images, etc.) to convey its meaning or feeling; aka non-linear; see also *Avant-garde*. Examples: René Clair's *Entr'acte* (1924), *Ballet Mecanique* (1924), Luis Buñuel's *Un Chien Andalou* (1928).

ABSURDISM, ABSURDIST — An art movement, stage, philosophical and literary term originally adopted by filmmakers, in which ordinary settings become bizarre, illogical, irrational, unrealistic, meaningless or incoherent for the purposes of describing the basic human condition as absurd. What make sense in a senseless world?

ACTING — When a person pretends to be a character in a play or screenplay.

ACT — A main division within the plot of a film; a film is often divided by "plot points" (places of dramatic change) rather than acts; long films are divided mid-way with an intermission.

ACTION — (1) any movement or series of events (usually rehearsed) that take place before the camera and propel the story forward toward its conclusion; (2) the word called out (by a megaphone) at the start of the current take during filming to alert actors to begin performing; (3) also refers to the main component of action films that often contain significant amounts of violence.

ACTOR — Refers to a performer, male or female, who plays a character role in a play or an on-screen film; alternate gender-neutral terms: player, artist or performer.

ACTRESS — Refers to any female who portrays a role in a play or screenplay.

ADAPTATION — The presentation of one art form through another medium; a film based upon, derived from (or adapted from) a stage play (or from another medium such as a short story, book, article, history, novel, video game, comic strip/book, etc.) which basically preserves both the setting and dialogue of the original; can be in the form of a script (screenplay) or a proposal treatment. *Who's Afraid of Virginia Woolf?* (1966) is a very faithful adaptation of Edward Albee's stage play of the same name; also, *Gone With The Wind* (1939) was adapted from Margaret Mitchell's novel, and *Apocalypse Now* (1979) was adapted from Joseph Conrad's novella *Heart of Darkness*.

AD-LIB — A line of dialogue improvised by an actor during a performance; can be either unscripted or deliberate; improvisation consists of ad-libbed dialogue (and action) that is invented or created by the performer.

ALAN SMITHEE FILM — The pseudonym used by directors who refuse to put their name on a film and want to disassociate themselves, usually when they believe their control or vision has been co-opted by the studio (i.e., the film could have been re-cut, mutilated and altered against their wishes); aka Alan Smithee Jr., Allan Smithee, or Allen Smithee. Examples: *Death of a Gunfighter* (1969), *Let's Get Harry* (1986), *The Shrimp on the Barbie* (1990), and the most recent film with the ironic alias: *An Alan Smithee Film: Burn, Hollywood, Burn* (1997).

A-LEVEL (or A-LIST) — usually refers to top-tier actors/actresses who are paid upwards of $20 million per feature film; can also refer to producers, directors and writers who can be guaranteed to have a film made and released. Examples: actors/ actresses Tom Hanks, Julia Roberts, Brad Pitt, Jodie Foster, or directors George Lucas and Steven Spielberg.

ALLEGORY — Mostly a literary term, but taken in film terms to mean a suggestive resemblance or correspondence between a visible event or character in a film with other more significant or abstract levels of meaning outside of the film; an extended metaphor. Examples: *Metropolis* (1927), *Animal Farm* (1955), *The Seventh Seal* (1957), *The Piano* (1993), *Eat Drink Man Woman* (1994), *The Matrix* (1999); also Biblical or Christ-related allegories.

ALLUSION — A direct or indirect reference, through an image or through dialogue, to the Bible, classic literature, a person, a place, an external and/or real-life event, another film, or a well-known cultural idea.

ALTERNATE ENDING — The shooting (or reshooting) of a film's ending for its theatrical release, usually enforced by the studio for any number of reasons (because of test audience preview results, controversial or unpopular subject matter, to provide a "happy" ending, etc.). Examples: *The Magnificent Ambersons* (1942), *Kiss Me Deadly* (1955), *Invasion of the Body Snatchers* (1956), *Blade Runner* (1982), *Little Shop of Horrors* (1986), *Fatal Attraction* (1987), and *Army of Darkness* (1993).

AMBIANCE — The feeling or mood of a particular scene or setting.

AMBIENT LIGHT — The natural light (usually soft) or surrounding light around a subject in a scene.

AMBIGUITY — A situation, storyline, scene or character, etc., in which there are apparent contradictions; an event (and its outcome) is deliberately left unclear, and there may exist more than one meaning or interpretation; can be either intentional or unintentional, to deliberately provoke imaginative thinking or confusion. Example: Robert Altman's *Three Women* (1977).

ANACHRONISM — An element or artifact in a film that belongs to another time or place; often anachronistic elements are called film flubs.

ANTAGONIST — The main character, person, group, society, nature, force, spirit world, bad guy, or villain of a film or script who is in adversarial conflict with the film's hero, lead character or protagonist; also sometimes termed the "Heavy."

ANTI-CLIMAX — Anything in a film, usually following the film's high point, zenith, apex, crescendo, or climax, in which there is an unsatisfying and disappointing let-down of emotion, or what is expected doesn't occur.

ANTI-HERO — The principal protagonist of a film who lacks the attributes or characteristics of a typical hero archetype, but with who the audience identifies. The character is often confused or conflicted with ambiguous morals or character defects and eccentricities, and lacks courage, honesty or grace. The anti-hero can be tough yet sympathetic, or display vulnerable and weak traits. Specifically, the anti-hero often functions outside the mainstream and challenges it.

ART DIRECTOR — Refers to the individual responsible for the design, look and feel of a film's set, including the number and type of props, furniture, windows, floors, ceilings dressings, and all other set materials; a member of the film's art department (responsible for set construction, interior design, and prop placement).

ARTHOUSE — A motion picture theater that shows foreign or non-mainstream independent films, often considered high-brow or "art" films.

ASPECT RATIO — In general, a term for how the image appears on the screen based on how it was shot; refers to the ratio of width (horizontal or top) to height (vertical or side) of a film frame, image or screen; the most common or standard aspect ratio in early films to the 1950s was called Academy Aperture (or ratio), at a ratio of 1.33:1 (the same as 4:3 on a television screen); normal 35mm films are shot at a ratio of 1.85:1; new widescreen formats and aspect ratios were introduced in the 1950s, from 1.65:1 and higher; CinemaScope (a trade name for a widescreen movie format used in the U.S. from 1953 to 1967) and other anamorphic systems (such as Panavision) have a 2.35:1 AR, while 70mm formats have an AR of 2.2:1; Cinerama had a 2.77:1 aspect ratio; letterboxed videos for widescreen TVs are frequently in 16:9 (or 1.77:1) AR.

AUDITION — The process whereby an actor-performer seeks a role by presenting to a director or casting director a prepared reading or by 'reading cold' from the film script, or performing a choreographed dance; after the initial audition, a performer may be called back for additional readings or run-throughs.

AUTOMATED DIALOGUE REPLACEMENT — ADR, Dialogue Looping. The re-recording of dialogue by actors in a sound studio during postproduction usually performed to playback of edited picture in order to match lip movements on screen. Replaces bad sound on location from background noise. Used to change the delivery or inflection of a line, or to insert new lines of dialogue placed against picture when we don't see the actor speaking.

AVANT-GARDE — Refers to an experimental, abstract, or highly independent, non-independent film that is often the forerunner of a new artistic genre or art form; avant-garde films self-consciously emphasize technique over substance; also loosely applies to a group of French and German filmmakers in the early 20th century and to some modern American experimental filmmakers (e.g., Andy Warhol), and their film movement that challenged conventional filmmaking; see also *Abstract Form*.

B

BEAT — Refers to an actor's term for how long to wait before doing an action; a beat is usually about one second. Sometimes, taking a moment. "Take a few beats before the line." Or, "Take a moment before you enter."

BELOW-THE-LINE EXPENSES — All physical production costs not included in the above-the-line expenses, including material costs, music rights, publicity, trailer, etc.

BIO-PIC, BIOGRAPHIC — A biographical film of the life of a famous personality or historical figure, particularly popularized by Warner Bros. in the 1930s; a sub-genre of drama and epic films. Examples: *The Story of Louis Pasteur* (1936), *The Life of Emile Zola* (1937), *Coal Miner's Daughter* (1980).

BIT PART (or BIT PLAYER) — A small acting role (usually only one scene, such as a waiter) with very few lines or acting; contrast to a cameo, extra, or "walk-on" role.

BLACK/DARK COMEDY — A type of comedy film, first popular during the late 1950s and early 1960s, in which normally serious subjects such as war, death, suffering or murder are treated with macabre humor and satire through iconography, dialogue and character; settings may include cemeteries, war rooms, funerals.

BLACKLISTING, BLACKLIST — Refers to late 1940s and early 1950s McCarthyism and the HUAC's (House Un-American Activities Committee) formal and informal discrimination and 'blacklisting' (effectively banning from employment) of various actors, artists and filmmakers based upon their personal, political, social or religious beliefs; the blacklist was a roster of artists who were not to be hired. The Hollywood Ten were a group of playwrights and moviemakers who refused to answer questions claiming their First Amendment rights, and were charged with contempt — they included Herbert Biberman, Lester Cole, Albert Maltz, Adrian Scott, Samuel Ornitz, Dalton Trumbo, Edward Dmytryk, Ring Lardner Jr., John Howard Lawson, and Alvah Bessie; also informally blacklisted recently were Jane Fonda and Vanessa Redgrave for outspoken attitudes.

BLAXPLOITATION — Use of the terms "black" and "exploitation." Mainly sensational, low-budget films in the 1970s featuring mostly African-American casts (and directors), that broke the mold of black characterization in feature films; usually emphasized fads of the time in hairstyles, music and costuming, and also brutality, sleazy sex, street life, racist and militant attitudes, etc.

BLOCKING — A process during which the director and actors determine where on the set the actors will move and stand, so that lighting and camera placements may be set; figuring out where the camera goes, how lights will be arranged, and actors' positions and movements — moment by moment — for each shot or take; staging of a film's movements are worked out by the director, often with stand-ins and the lighting crew before actual shooting

BLUE SCREEN — Special effects process whereby actors work in front of an evenly lit, monochromatic (usually blue or green) background or screen. The background is replaced (or matted) in postproduction by chroma-keying or optical printer, allowing other footage or computer-generated images to form the image. Common to see use of blue chroma key for film stock, and green for digital capture.

BODY DOUBLE — Performers or actors who take the place of a lead actor in scenes that require a close-up of body parts without the face visible, often for nude scenes requiring exposed close-ups (considered distasteful by some actors), or scenes requiring physical fitness.

BOUNCE CARD — Disc or card for bouncing light onto a subject. Also used to brighten shadows.

BUZZ TRACK — A soundtrack of natural, atmospheric, on-location background noise that is added to the re-recorded (or looped) track of actors' dialogue and other sound effects recordings to create a more realistic sound; a wild track or sound refers to a soundtrack w/o any synchronized picture accompanying it (e.g., the sounds of a playground).

C

CALL SHEET — Daily agenda/schedule distributed to all department heads and key staff. Not typically given to background or Day Players, keeping personal information tight and to let every department know when to arrive and where they report.

CAMEO — Originally meaning "a small piece of artwork," refers to a bit part (usually a brief, non-speaking or "walk-on" role that is uncredited or unbilled) or special screen appearance by a famous actor, director or prominent person who would ordinarily not take such a small part; also refers to a type of camera shot in which the subject is filmed against a black or neutral background.

CARICATURE — a character appearing ridiculously out of proportion because of one physical, psychological or moral trait that has been grossly or broadly exaggerated; a caricature often portrays a character in an unrealistic, stereotypical fashion.

CAST — The group of performers assembled for the purposed of acting out a play or screenplay, organized by the size of the respective roles; leads with speaking roles, and supporting characters or seconds, bit players, featured extras and background players or extras.

CAST AGAINST TYPE — An actor playing a role distinctly different from roles previously played.

CASTING — The process of selecting and hiring actors to play the roles and characters in a film production. Lead roles are typically cast or selected by the director or a producer, and the minor or supporting roles and bit parts by a casting director.

CASTING COUCH — Refers to the illegal practice (mostly during the heyday of the studio system) when unknown young actors or actresses exchanged sex (literally on an office couch) with a casting director or producer in order to acquire/land a role in a film.

CAST OF THOUSANDS — An advertising claim, often used in big-screen historical epics of the 1930s-60s, when literally thousands of extras were hired for crowd scenes, battle scenes, etc.

CHARACTER — The fictitious or real individual in a story, portrayed by an actor.

CHARACTER COLOR CODING — Refers to identifying a film's character or persona with a particular color; changes in color often represent transformations, shifts, merges, or changes in persona. Examples: the explicit naming of the characters by color in Quentin Tarantino's *Reservoir Dogs* (1992); also the color-coded couples in Kenneth Branagh's *Love's Labour's Lost* (2000).

CHARACTER STUDY — A film that uses strong characterizations, interactions and the personalities of its characters to tell a story, with plot and narrative almost secondary to them.

CHEAT — When providing a different angle, to cheat toward lens, or set up a shot to cheat the eyeline to match angles.

CHEATER CUT — The footage put into the beginning of a serial episode to show what happened at the end of the previous episode.

CHEMISTRY (or SCREEN CHEMISTRY) — Referring to performances between actors who are uncommonly suited and perfectly complementary to each other. Examples: Spencer Tracy and

Katharine Hepburn, Fred Astaire and Ginger Rogers, Jack Lemmon and Walter Matthau, Elizabeth Taylor and Richard Burton, Stan Laurel and Oliver Hardy, Mel Gibson and Danny Glover.

CHIAROSCURO — Literally, the combination of the two Italian words for "clear/bright" and "dark;" refers to a notable, contrasting use of light and shade in scenes; often achieved by using a spotlight; this film lighting technique had its roots in German Expressionistic cinematography.

CLEAN SPEECH — Getting through the dialogue with perfect delivery. No overhead noises to cut or wait for, or overlapping words to complicate editing. Lines begin and end clearly.

CUTAWAY — Editing to a new view within a scene sequence. Close-up or wide. Used to break up a matching action sequence, fix bad continuity or coverage.

CUE — Any sign or signal to start an action, an entrance, a line or a camera move in a shot sequence. "Pick up your cues," generally means to remove the air space from the end of one line to the beginning of another, increasing the speed of delivery of lines.

D

DIRECTING — The art of combining all the elements of filmmaking into a whole, arranging the action being filmed during the production of a movie and making certain that the action and the spoken word relates to the content and context of the screenplay.

DIRECTOR — The one who does all of the above.

DOLLY SHOT — A shot where the camera is placed on a dolly truck or track and is moved while filming. Also known as a tracking shot.

E

EYE LINE — Direction an actor looks off-screen to match a reverse angle or a P.O.V. shot.

F

FRAME LINE — The edges of any shot, from extreme close-up to wide establishing. Also space between frames.

H

HEAD ROOM — The space between the top of a subject's head and the top of the frame. Headroom must be carefully apportioned so that there is not too much or too little, especially if shooting for transfer to video or for blowup, where the frame will be cropped in a little on the top and sides.

HIT THE MARK (or MAKE YOUR MARK, TAKE YOUR MARK) — Instructions to an actor where to begin and end blocking points within a setup. To "hit the mark" means to land where you need to be with regard to the frame line.

I

IMPROVISE — A rehearsal technique allowing actors to make up their action and lines. No script, no rehearsals, actors work with a setup of the scene's intention. Lends to spontaneity and surprise moments which access their own emotional content. Origins with the *Commedia dell'Arte* street performers of the Italian Renaissance, using stock/type characters and standard scene setups.

L

LOOPING — Film on a loop while the actor matches the dialogue in postproduction.

M

MARTINI SHOT — Last shot of the day. Frequently turns into the Abby Singer. See *Abby Singer*. Time to get your cocktails up.

MASTER SHOT — A single shot, usually a wide shot, that incorporates the whole scene from beginning to end. Typically a master shot will be filmed first, and then all the close-ups and other shots afterwards.

M.O.S. — A shot, a sequence or film that is shot without sound, which is added later. Stands for "Mit Out Sound," and derives from an old Hollywood story about a German director asking for a shot to be filmed "mit out sound," and the camera assistant complying with this request by writing "M.O.S." on the slate.

METHOD ACTING — A realistic acting style, founded by Konstantin Stanislavski, incorporating common experiences within the actor and the character and the use of actions and objectives.

N

NOSE ROOM — When a subject is in profile, nose room is the space between their face and the edge of the frame. In a profile shot, nose room is considered "good" when there's a little extra room in front of the person's face, rather than behind their head. The general rule is that the space around the subject should be apportioned to 2/3 in front of the subject's head, and 1/3 behind.

P

PACE — Tempo at which the storyline of a film unfolds including action, the length of scenes, camera angles, color levels, editing, lighting, composition and sound. See *Timing*.

PHOTO DOUBLE — Someone dressed to look like an actor when the actor isn't really there; usually long shots, shots of hands or legs, etc. Don't confuse with *Stand In*.

PICKUP — Describes shots to cover any material left out and shot in postproduction after editors discover something missing and needed. Also called reshoot. Also used in production to describe picking up dialogue in the middle of a setup when the director doesn't say "cut," keeps the camera rolling, actors pick up the lines and keep going.

P.O.V. Shot — Point of View from the character's perspective, as if the audience were seeing the scene; paired with a *Reaction Shot* to establish the P.O.V.

R

Rack Focus — When focus is changed while shooting to shift attention from one thing to another. Unlike a Follow Focus shot, which is keeping someone in focus.

Read-through — Early rehearsal where the entire cast and key designers and crew gather to hear the script read. Usually followed with discussions and libations. Can kick off the rehearsal process and serve as a way to build a team. A time for celebration, concentration, and clear vision for your entire shoot.

Retake — A reshoot of part or all of a previously completed scene to fix something or improve upon what was already shot.

Role descriptions for Television and Film —

TELEVISION

Series Regular: You play a main character on a television series and appear in almost every episode of the season.

Guest Star: You play a character that has a significant part in the storyline of an episode and you would likely appear in multiple scenes. Your name will appear in the opening credits.

Co-star: You play a supporting role and have less dialogue than a guest star. You are likely in one scene and your character is there to support the main characters and help move along the storyline. Your name will appear in the closing credits.

Recurring: You play a character that appears in more than one episode. This can be a guest-starring role or co-starring role.

UNDER-FIVE: You have a role with less than five lines. At times, these roles can be bumped up to co-star.

FEATURED: You do not have lines but your role is given special focus.

EXTRA: You do not have lines and are in the background of scenes.

FILM
LEAD: You play a main character in a film.

SUPPORTING: You play a significant character in a film and your role supports the lead characters.

CAMEO: You are a well-known celebrity playing a smaller role.

DAY Player: You have a small part that is usually shot in one day.

S

SHOOTING SCRIPT — Final approved script in chronological order used in the production of a motion picture. Followed by all staff, crew and actors, it contains dialogue, action cues, the breakdown of the scenes and all required shots. Used to create daily shooting schedules.

SHOOTING SCHEDULE — Contains all cast and crew call times, locations, equipment, meal breaks, weather reports, sunrise and sunset, and any other important information required for a day's shoot. Keeps the team on track when scenes are filmed out of sequence and out of a continuous line of progression. Similar to a call sheet.

STAND-IN — People who resemble the stars of the film in height and coloring and "stand in" for an actor while the set is being readied with lighting and camera position.

T

TIMING — Pace or rhythm of the delivery of lines and physical action. Also used in editing to achieve rhythm. Dramas tend to have a slower timing than comic films where "timing is everything."

TRACKING SHOT — When the camera is placed on a dolly and moves while rolling. See *Dolly Shot*.

TYPECASTING — Filling roles with actors who fit a stereotype. Recognizable character types. An actor who becomes known for playing a type, as in action hero or romantic lead, is said to be *cast against type* when landing a role they're not normally known for.

U

UPSTAGE — Drawing attention away from the focal point or person. To walk between the camera and the star, to attract attention to yourself inappropriately.

W

WRAP or "IT'S A WRAP!" — Said at the end of the day, or on the entire film.

THE PARTS OF SPEECH

VERBS

To Schmooze: befriend scum
To Pitch: grovel shamelessly
To Brainstorm: feign preparedness
To Research: procrastinate indefinitely
To Network: spread misinformation
To Collaborate: argue incessantly
To Freelance: collect unemployment

NOUNS

Agent = frustrated lawyer
Lawyer = frustrated producer
Producer = frustrated writer
Writer = frustrated director
Director = frustrated actor
Actor = frustrated human

COMPOUND WORDS

High Concept = Low Brow
Production Value = Gore
Entry Level = Pays nothing
Highly Qualified = Knows the producer

FINANCIAL TERMS

Net: Something that apparently doesn't exist
Gross: Studio executives' salaries
Back End: You're a fool if you think you'll ever see it.
Residuals: Braces for your kids
Deferral: Don't hold your breath
Points: See *Net* and *Back End*

COMMON PHRASES

You can trust me = You must be new
It needs some polish = Change everything
It shows promise = It stinks rotten
It needs some fine-tuning = Change everything
I'd like some input = I want total control
It needs some honing = Change everything
Call me back next week = Stay out of my life
It needs some tightening = Change everything
Try and punch it up = I have no idea what I want
It needs some streamlining = Change everything
You'll never work in this town again = I have no power
whatsoever

BIBLIOGRAPHY AND RESOURCES

CHAPTER ONE: SAVE MONEY — DO IT YOURSELF

showbizdata.com/
showbizdata.com/worldbox.cfm
davidworthfilm.com

CHAPTER TWO: YOUR DIRECTING CAREER

withoutabox.com, a division of *imdb.com*
theactorscenter.org

CHAPTER FOUR: INDUSTRY STANDARDS

Kari Wishingrad: *starsagency.com, kariwishingrad.net*
Photo credit: Stuart Locklear, *stuartlocklearphotography.com*

Stephanie Carwin: *stephaniecarwin.com*
Photo credit: Playbox Studios: The Photography of Bradley K. Ross, *playboxstudios.com*

Mary Garcia: *mgsprag002@msn.com,*
Photo credit: Matthew Karas Photography, *mattkaras.com*

Shawn-Caulin Young: *shawncaulinyoung.com*
Manager, Tina Treadwell, *tinatreadwell@mac.com*
Photo credit: Michael D'Ambrosia, *michaeldambrosia.com*

Fred Pitts: *fredpitts@gmail.com*

JE Talent, *jetalent.com, john@jetalent.com, deedee@jetalent.com*

Photo credit: Stuart Locklear, *stuartlocklearphotography.com*

André Mathieu: Tonry Talent, *tonry@tonrytalent.com*

Photo credit: Rod Goodman, *rodgoodmanphoto.com*

Jim Johnson, *studio7photo.com*

Maxine Greco: *tagtalent.com, maxinegreco.com*

Photo credit: Chadd Green, PrimaDonna Productions, Inc. *primadonnaproductions.com*

CHAPTER FIVE: ACTING — WHAT IS IT?

Justice Potter Stewart, concurring opinion in Jacobellis v. Ohio 378 U.S. 184 (1964), regarding possible obscenity in *The Lovers*.

CHAPTER SIX: TIMELINES —
WHEN TO START AND WHAT TO DO BEFORE JUMPING IN

Judith Weston's *Directing Actors*, 2nd edition. Michael Wiese Productions, 2010.

CHAPTER SEVEN: THE CASTING BREAKDOWN —
SPREADING THE WORD

Breakdown Services — *breakdownservices.com*

Actors Access — *actorsaccess.com*

Now Casting — *nowcasting.com*

Casting Networks — *castingnetworks.com*

Mandy — *mandy.com*

Bay Area Casting News — *bayareacasting.com*

New England Film — *nefilm.com*

Oregon Media Production Association — *ompa.com*
Media Match — *media-match.com*

CHAPTER ELEVEN: OFFERS AND CONTRACTS

Free Legal Documents — *free-legal-document.com*

CHAPTER FOURTEEN: SO YOU WANT TO BE A CASTING DIRECTOR

Casting Society of America — *castingsociety.com*
Oregon Media Producers Association — *ompa.org*
Massachusetts Film Office — *mafilm.org*
New England Film — *newenglandfilm.com*
San Francisco — *reeldirectory.com*
Chicago Film Office — *chicagofilms.org*
Illinois Film Office — *illinoisfilm.biz*
Dallas Film Office — *filmdfw.com*
California Film Office — *film.ca.gov*
New York City Film Office — *nyc.gov/html/film/html/index/index.shtml*

BOOK JACKET CONTACTS:

KARI NEVIL, WRITER, DIRECTOR

Kari Nevil started her career in the entertainment industry while working with recording artists at EMI and Capitol Records. She transitioned to film at Disney Studios before moving back to San Francisco to found JuneBug Productions for music and video projects. JuneBug Films, Incorporated, was created as the feature and documentary arm, where Nevil has produced, directed and written award-winning projects with an emphasis on strengthening the images of women on film. Nevil serves on multiple festival juries, is a consultant to other filmmakers and continues to develop projects, which inspire and educate. Her new feature film is a rock and roll romantic comedy, and her ongoing documentaries range from complicated subjects such as infidelity, teen sexuality and adoption. Her company's motto is: "Make the Movie," to which she adds, "with Integrity."

junebugfilms.com
PO Box 620137
Woodside, CA 94062.0137
(650) 728-2000 Studio
(650) 888-6407 Mobile

NANCI GAGLIO, WRITER, DIRECTOR
Nanci Gaglio is a New York and San Francisco based writer and director. Her short films have screened in dozens of film festivals around the world. Nanci has a television series in development with BBC London, and is the past screenwriting instructor at UC Berkeley Extension. *Fredericka* is her newest short film, based on her own short story. US phone: (415) 786-9499

KARI WISHINGRAD, ACTRESS, PRODUCER
kwish@vom.com
Kari Wishingrad is an actress and producer living in the San Francisco Bay Area with experience in film, voice over, commercials, print, television and stage.
kariwishingrad.net

PAUL MARTIN, DIRECTOR
paul@vineyardproductions.com
Paul Martin is a writer/director with twenty years in the film industry. He founded Vineyard Productions, producing and directing short films. He wrote and directed the award-winning short *Ash Wednesday*. *Flashcards*, a narrative on child abuse, was selected for the "Marche Du Film" at Cannes. Screenplays include *Rockets Red Glare* and *Two Moons*, which have received recognition at national screenplay competitions.

Stephen Kopels, founder — San Francisco School of Digital Filmmaking
Stephen Kopels has been a working filmmaker for 40 years. Starting as a combat photographer in Vietnam, his career has included 12 years as Senior Producer/Director for PBS, 30 years as a commercial and documentary director and director of photography. Stephen is Founder and President of The San Francisco School of Digital Filmmaking and Fog City Pictures. *sfdigifilm.com*

Ken Lazer, casting director
Ken Lazer has nearly 20 years of professional experience casting television commercials, television series, feature films, webisodes, infomercials, industrials and voice overs. He is known by his clients for his acute eye to cast the right talent for any project. Actors know him for his outgoing personality and insightful direction making them feel relaxed and able to enjoy the audition process. Over the years, Ken has cast for hundreds of national, international, regional and local commercials and voice overs for numerous top brand name clients as well as earned screen credits for feature films and television series. He lives in New York City.
info@kenlazercasting.com
Ken Lazer Casting
(646) 781-9182
kenlazercasting.com

Robert Pickett, writer, director, actor
Robert Pickett has been writing and doing theatre since he could speak and write, writing plays based on fairy tales and performing them in the family garage. He received his MFA and BA in Theatre Directing and an AA in Acting. He has written three feature length screenplays, several shorts, as well as a musical, one acts, and a comic tragedy for the theatre.
divinemadness99@hotmail.com

Candy Campbell, writer, producer, director, MSN, RN
Candy Campbell is an award-winning filmmaker, author, educator, actress, comedienne and registered nurse who made her television debut on NBC's *Trauma*. Ms. Campbell produced and directed the award-winning documentary film, *Micropremature Babies: How Low Can You Go?* Contact her at: *candycampbell.com* or *candythenurse.com*, *peripateticproductions .com*, *periprod@aol.com*

Sarah Kliban, actress, casting director — International Talent Casting, *diversitycasting.com*
P.O. Box 330104 San Francisco, CA 94133, (415) 781-2278, *casting@value.net*

ABOUT THE AUTHOR

Photo credit: Owen Carey, owencareyphoto.com

Hester Schell is a master acting teacher, writer, producer, stage and film director, actor, mentor and coach. Her academic background includes: Professor of Theatre Arts at De Anza College in California, where she pioneered the film acting and stand-up comedy programs; Adjunct Professor of Theatre: Notre Dame de Namur University. Guest Faculty: University of London, San Francisco's Film Arts Foundation, and The San Francisco School of Digital Filmmaking. Recent plays and screenplays: *Colony Collapse, The Dark Room, Soul's Messenger,* and *A Cup Of Coffee,* written for the New England Russian Theatre Festival. Recent directing: Provincetown Playwrights Festival, New England Russian Theatre Festival. Shorts: *Ju$T Under A Million* (narrative comedy), which premiered at the Beverly Hills High Definition Film Festival and airing on cable in Austin, Dallas and Atlanta on the Hottv channel; *Blankets For Afghanistan* (documentary), broadcast through Free Speech TV. Other film festivals include: Cannes, CineQuest, San Francisco International Film Festival, Rochester and Boston Film Festivals and others. In 2010, Hester served as Associate Producer for *Bait and Switch TV: Investigative*

Satire (baitandswitchtv.com). Career highlights include touring England with the award-winning puppet company Lunatique Fantastique and representing the U.S. at the International Children's Theatre Festival in Russia. Hester is a member of the Screen Actors Guild, the American Federation of Television and Radio Artists, and the Harvard Square Screen Writers. Speaking engagements include the Connecticut Screenwriters Association, San Francisco Chapter of IndieClub and San Francisco Black-American Film Festival.

Master of Fine Arts: University of Utah; Bachelor of Arts: Portland State University; Associates of Arts: American Academy of Dramatic Arts in New York. Conservatory training: Trinity Square Repertory Theatre Conservatory, Providence, Rhode Island.

Hester has been casting plays, short films and features throughout her career and is available for workshops and seminars on a variety of topics. Contact her at *hester.schell@ gmail.com*, LinkedIn or Facebook.

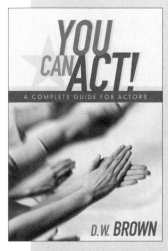

YOU CAN ACT!
A COMPLETE GUIDE FOR ACTORS

D.W. BROWN

What do Jamie Kennedy, Keanu Reeves, Sean Penn, Dustin Hoffman, and Robert DeNiro have in common? They were all coached by or participated in seminars with D.W. Brown — master acting teacher.

You Can Act! describes, with humor and inspiration, every detail necessary for fulfilling any role you might be called upon to perform. Beyond that, it provides extensive tips and reference material for many specialized situations, whether playing comedy or negotiating all manner of stage business; performing the part of a character with insanity or one with a gunshot wound. *You Can Act!* also offers a philosophical approach to performing that unites you with the artists through the ages.

"Working with D .W. Brown is the most important thing I have done for my career. D. W. has a gentle, disarming way about him which helped me break down my social veneers and limitations, and allowed me to expand my capabilities as an actress. This method gave me a road map to follow and all of the tools I needed to continue to develop my instincts so I could take on any role and feel confident about it."
> — Sharon Case, *The Young and the Restless,* five time nominated and winner of the Daytime Emmy for Outstanding Supporting Actress

"D. W. Brown trains beginning actors and makes them working actors, and he takes working actors and makes them stars."
> — Valerie McCaffrey, Head of Casting for New Line Cinema

As artistic head of The Joanne Baron/ D. W. Brown Studio (*www.baronbrown.com*), D. W. BROWN has trained, directed, and coached hundreds of actors and led seminars on acting with Sean Penn, Benicio Del Toro, Anthony Hopkins, Dustin Hoffman, Susan Sarandon, and Sidney Pollack; other notables who have spoken at the studio include Robert De Niro, Jim Caviezel, Jeff Goldblum, Martin Sheen, Richard Dreyfuss, John Singleton, Martha Coolidge, Robert Towne, and Mark Rydell.

D. W. has personally coached and taught Robin Wright Penn, Leslie Mann, Keanu Reeves, Michael Richards, Jamie Kennedy, Nicollette Sheridan, Michael Vartan, Jenny Garth, directors Sam Raimi and Tom Shadyac, and many other great talents. He has just finished writing and directing the feature film *In Northwood* starring Nick Stahl, Olivia Wilde, Dash Mihok, Pruit Taylor Vince, and Shoreh Aghdashloo (Academy® Award nominee for *House of Sand and Fog*).

$24.95 · 350 PAGES · ORDER NUMBER 126RLS · ISBN: 9781932907568

DIRECTING ACTORS
CREATING MEMORABLE PERFORMANCES
FOR FILM AND TELEVISION

JUDITH WESTON

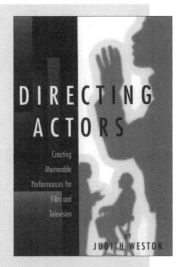

BEST SELLER
OVER 45,000 COPIES SOLD!

Directing film or television is a high-stakes occupation. It captures your full attention at every moment, calling on you to commit every resource and stretch yourself to the limit. It's the white-water rafting of entertainment jobs. But for many directors, the excitement they feel about a new project tightens into anxiety when it comes to working with actors.

This book provides a method for establishing creative, collaborative relationships with actors, getting the most out of rehearsals, troubleshooting poor performances, giving briefer directions, and much more. It addresses what actors want from a director, what directors do wrong, and constructively analyzes the director-actor relationship.

"Judith Weston is an extraordinarily gifted teacher."
> — David Chase, Emmy® Award-Winning Writer,
> Director, and Producer *The Sopranos,*
> *Northern Exposure, I'll Fly Away*

"I believe that working with Judith's ideas and principles has been the most useful time I've spent preparing for my work. I think that if Judith's book were mandatory reading for all directors, the quality of the director-actor process would be transformed, and better drama would result."
> — John Patterson, Director
> *Six Feet Under, CSI: Crime Scene Investigation,*
> *The Practice, Law and Order*

"I know a great teacher when I find one! Everything in this book is brilliant and original and true."
> — Polly Platt, Producer, *Bottle Rocket*
> Executive Producer, *Broadcast News, The War of the Roses*

JUDITH WESTON was a professional actor for 20 years and has taught Acting for Directors for over a decade.

$26.95 · 314 PAGES · ORDER NUMBER 4RLS · ISBN: 0941188248

DIRECTING FEATURE FILMS
THE CREATIVE COLLABORATION BETWEEN DIRECTORS, WRITERS, AND ACTORS

MARK TRAVIS

The director is the guide, the inspiration, the focus that can shepherd hundreds of artists through the most chaotic, complex collaboration imaginable. But how does one person draw all these individuals together to realize a single vision?

Directing Feature Films takes you through the entire creative process of filmmaking – from concept to completion. You will learn how to really read a script, find its core, determine your vision, and effectively communicate with writers, actors, designers, cinematographers, editors, composers, and all the members of your creative team to ensure that vision reaches the screen.

This edition of the best-selling *The Director's Journey* contains new material on all aspects of filmmaking, taking the reader even deeper into the process.

"A comprehensive and inspired examination of craft. A must read for any serious professional."
   – Mark Rydell, Director, *On Golden Pond, James Dean*

"Mark Travis is the only practical teacher of directing I've ever met – and simply the best. I learned more from him than I did in four years of film school."
         – Cyrus Nowrasteh, Writer/Director
           The Day Reagan Was Shot

"With astonishing clarity Mark Travis articulates the techniques and skills of film directing."
         – John Badham, Director,
           Saturday Night Fever, War Games, Blue Thunder

MARK TRAVIS has directed motion pictures, television programs, and stage shows. A graduate of the Yale School of Drama, Mark has shared his techniques on directing in courses around the world. He has served as a directing consultant on many feature films and top-rated television series.

$26.95 · 402 PAGES · ORDER NUMBER 96RLS · ISBN: 9780941188432

 # THE MYTH OF MWP

In a dark time, a light bringer came along, leading the curious and the frustrated to clarity and empowerment. It took the well-guarded secrets out of the hands of the few and made them available to all. It spread a spirit of openness and creative freedom, and built a storehouse of knowledge dedicated to the betterment of the arts.

The essence of the Michael Wiese Productions (MWP) is empowering people who have the burning desire to express themselves creatively. We help them realize their dreams by putting the tools in their hands. We demystify the sometimes secretive worlds of screenwriting, directing, acting, producing, film financing, and other media crafts.

By doing so, we hope to bring forth a realization of 'conscious media' which we define as being positively charged, emphasizing hope and affirming positive values like trust, cooperation, self-empowerment, freedom, and love. Grounded in the deep roots of myth, it aims to be healing both for those who make the art and those who encounter it. It hopes to be transformative for people, opening doors to new possibilities and pulling back veils to reveal hidden worlds.

MWP has built a storehouse of knowledge unequaled in the world, for no other publisher has so many titles on the media arts. Please visit www.mwp.com where you will find many free resources and a 25% discount on our books. Sign up and become part of the wider creative community!

Onward and upward,

Michael Wiese
Publisher/Filmmaker

FILM & VIDEO BOOKS

SCREENWRITING | WRITING

And the Best Screenplay Goes to... | Dr. Linda Seger | $26.95
Archetypes for Writers | Jennifer Van Bergen | $22.95
Bali Brothers | Lacy Waltzman, Matthew Bishop, Michael Wiese | $12.95
Cinematic Storytelling | Jennifer Van Sijll | $24.95
Could It Be a Movie? | Christina Hamlett | $26.95
Creating Characters | Marisa D'Vari | $26.95
Crime Writer's Reference Guide, The | Martin Roth | $20.95
Deep Cinema | Mary Trainor-Brigham | $19.95
Elephant Bucks | Sheldon Bull | $24.95
Fast, Cheap & Written That Way | John Gaspard | $26.95
Hollywood Standard – 2nd Edition, The | Christopher Riley | $18.95
Horror Screenwriting | Devin Watson | $24.95
I Could've Written a Better Movie than That! | Derek Rydall | $26.95
Inner Drives | Pamela Jaye Smith | $26.95
Moral Premise, The | Stanley D. Williams, Ph.D. | $24.95
Myth and the Movies | Stuart Voytilla | $26.95
Power of the Dark Side, The | Pamela Jaye Smith | $22.95
Psychology for Screenwriters | William Indick, Ph.D. | $26.95
Reflections of the Shadow | Jeffrey Hirschberg | $26.95
Rewrite | Paul Chitlik | $16.95
Romancing the A-List | Christopher Keane | $18.95
Save the Cat! | Blake Snyder | $19.95
Save the Cat! Goes to the Movies | Blake Snyder | $24.95
Screenwriting 101 | Neill D. Hicks | $16.95
Screenwriting for Teens | Christina Hamlett | $18.95
Script-Selling Game, The | Kathie Fong Yoneda | $16.95
Stealing Fire From the Gods, 2nd Edition | James Bonnet | $26.95
Talk the Talk | Penny Penniston | $24.95
Way of Story, The | Catherine Ann Jones | $22.95
What Are You Laughing At? | Brad Schreiber | $19.95
Writer's Journey – 3rd Edition, The | Christopher Vogler | $26.95
Writer's Partner, The | Martin Roth | $24.95
Writing the Action Adventure Film | Neill D. Hicks | $14.95
Writing the Comedy Film | Stuart Voytilla & Scott Petri | $14.95
Writing the Killer Treatment | Michael Halperin | $14.95
Writing the Second Act | Michael Halperin | $19.95
Writing the Thriller Film | Neill D. Hicks | $14.95
Writing the TV Drama Series, 2nd Edition | Pamela Douglas | $26.95
Your Screenplay Sucks! | William M. Akers | $19.95

FILMMAKING

Film School | Richard D. Pepperman | $24.95
Power of Film, The | Howard Suber | $27.95

PITCHING

Perfect Pitch – 2nd Edition, The | Ken Rotcop | $19.95
Selling Your Story in 60 Seconds | Michael Hauge | $12.95

SHORTS

Filmmaking for Teens, 2nd Edition | Troy Lanier & Clay Nichols | $24.95
Making It Big in Shorts | Kim Adelman | $22.95

BUDGET | PRODUCTION MANAGEMENT

Film & Video Budgets, 5th Updated Edition | Deke Simon | $26.95
Film Production Management 101 | Deborah S. Patz | $39.95

DIRECTING | VISUALIZATION

Animation Unleashed | Ellen Besen | $26.95

Cinematography for Directors | Jacqueline Frost | $29.95
Citizen Kane Crash Course in Cinematography | David Worth | $19.95
Directing Actors | Judith Weston | $26.95
Directing Feature Films | Mark Travis | $26.95
Fast, Cheap & Under Control | John Gaspard | $26.95
Film Directing: Cinematic Motion, 2nd Edition | Steven D. Katz | $27.95
Film Directing: Shot by Shot | Steven D. Katz | $27.95
Film Director's Intuition, The | Judith Weston | $26.95
First Time Director | Gil Bettman | $27.95
From Word to Image, 2nd Edition | Marcie Begleiter | $26.95
I'll Be in My Trailer! | John Badham & Craig Modderno | $26.95
Master Shots | Christopher Kenworthy | $24.95
Setting Up Your Scenes | Richard D. Pepperman | $24.95
Setting Up Your Shots, 2nd Edition | Jeremy Vineyard | $22.95
Working Director, The | Charles Wilkinson | $22.95

DIGITAL | DOCUMENTARY | SPECIAL

Digital Filmmaking 101, 2nd Edition | Dale Newton & John Gaspard | $26.95
Digital Moviemaking 3.0 | Scott Billups | $24.95
Digital Video Secrets | Tony Levelle | $26.95
Greenscreen Made Easy | Jeremy Hanke & Michele Yamazaki | $19.95
Producing with Passion | Dorothy Fadiman & Tony Levelle | $22.95
Special Effects | Michael Slone | $31.95

EDITING

Cut by Cut | Gael Chandler | $35.95
Cut to the Chase | Bobbie O'Steen | $24.95
Eye is Quicker, The | Richard D. Pepperman | $27.95
Film Editing | Gael Chandler | $34.95
Invisible Cut, The | Bobbie O'Steen | $28.95

SOUND | DVD | CAREER

Complete DVD Book, The | Chris Gore & Paul J. Salamoff | $26.95
Costume Design 101, 2nd Edition | Richard La Motte | $24.95
Hitting Your Mark, 2nd Edition | Steve Carlson | $22.95
Sound Design | David Sonnenschein | $19.95
Sound Effects Bible, The | Ric Viers | $26.95
Storyboarding 101 | James Fraioli | $19.95
There's No Business Like Soul Business | Derek Rydall | $22.95
You Can Act! | D.W. Brown | $24.95

FINANCE | MARKETING | FUNDING

Art of Film Funding, The | Carole Lee Dean | $26.95
Bankroll | Tom Malloy | $26.95
Complete Independent Movie Marketing Handbook, The | Mark Steven Bosko | $39.95
Getting the Money | Jeremy Jusso | $26.95
Independent Film and Videomakers Guide – 2nd Edition, The | Michael Wiese | $29.95
Independent Film Distribution | Phil Hall | $26.95
Shaking the Money Tree, 3rd Edition | Morrie Warshawski | $26.95

MEDITATION | ART

Mandalas of Bali | Dewa Nyoman Batuan | $39.95

OUR FILMS

Dolphin Adventures: DVD | Michael Wiese and Hardy Jones | $24.95
Hardware Wars: DVD | Written and Directed by Ernie Fosselius | $14.95
On the Edge of a Dream | Michael Wiese | $16.95
Sacred Sites of the Dalai Lamas– DVD, The | Documentary by Michael Wiese | $24.95